Islam and Sikhism

PATRICIA WATSON & ROBERT McVEIGH

Series Editor: Robert McVeigh

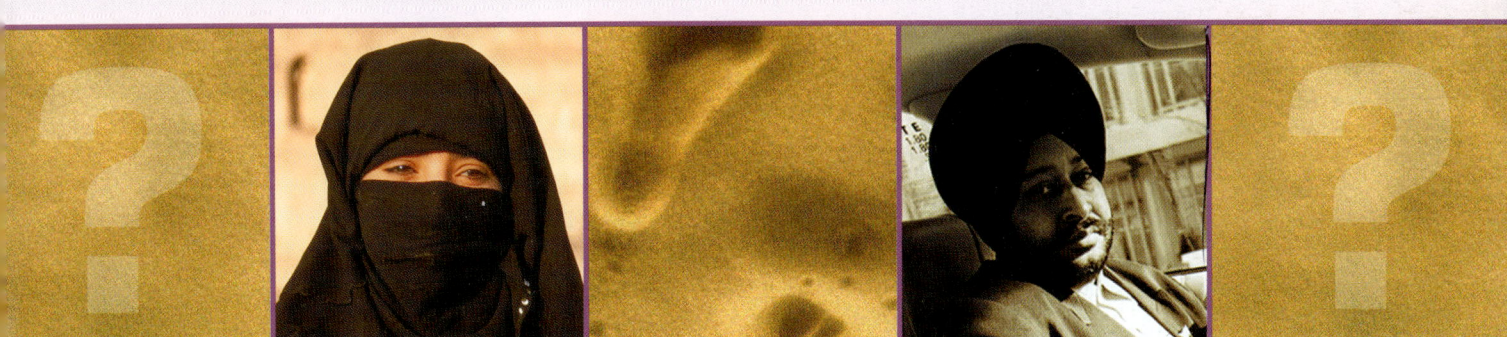

Hodder Gibson
A MEMBER OF THE HODDER HEADLINE GROUP

The Publishers would like to thank the following for permission to reproduce copyright material:

Photo credits p.3 © ATEF HASSAN/Reuters/Corbis; p.4 © Sophie Elbaz/Sygma/Corbis (top); © Earl & Nazima Kowall/CORBIS (bottom); p.12 AHMAD AL-RUBAYE/AFP/Getty Images; p.13 ArkReligion.com/Alamy; p.14 © Kazuyoshi Nomachi/Corbis; p.15 Muhannad Fala'ah/Getty Images; p.19 © ANDANSON JAMES/CORBIS SYGMA; p.25 © David Lees/CORBIS; p.28 Ferruccio/Alamy; p.30 Ersoy Emin/Alamy (left); World Religions Picture Library (centre); BEHROUZ MEHRI/AFP/Getty Images (right); p.31 Photodisc (top left); Imageshop/Alamy (top right); INSADCO Photography/Alamy (bottom left); ArkReligion.com/Alamy (bottom right); p.36 World Religions Picture Library; p.40 ArkReligion.com/Alamy; p.42 © Kazuyoshi Nomachi/Corbis (top); ArkReligion.com/Alamy (bottom); p.43 Muhannad Fala'ah/Getty Images (top); © Kazuyoshi Nomachi/Corbis (bottom); p.46 © ALI HAIDER/epa/Corbis; p.51 Anjum Naveed/AP Photo/Empics; p.53 © Mona Reeder/Dallas Morning News/Corbis (top); Alex Segre/Alamy (bottom); p.57 ATTA KENARE/AFP/Getty Images (top); World Religions Photo Library/Alamy (bottom); p.63 © DESAI NOSHIR/CORBIS SYGMA; p.69 Paul Doyle/Alamy; p.72 Paul Doyle/Alamy; p.75 © World Religions Photo Library/Alamy; p.78 World Religions Photo Library/Alamy (top); ArkReligion.com/Alamy (bottom); p.79 SCPhotos/Alamy; p.86 World Religions Photo Library/Alamy; p.88 ArkReligion.com/Alamy (top); © Religious Education, University of Strathclyde (bottom); p.89 Nikreates/Alamy (left); Canadian Press, Adrian Wyld/AP Photo/Empics (right); p.93 © Dave Bartruff/CORBIS; p.95 ArkReligion.com/Alamy; p.99 www.shrg.org; p.106 Dominic Burke/Alamy; p.109 and 110 Pingalwara, www.pingalwaraonline.org (all).

Acknowledgements p.6 Religious materials about the benefits of fasting is reproduced courtesy of http://submission.org; p.8/9 Extracted from The Big Issue in Scotland, October 20–26, 2005; p.10/11 Ramadan song and Ramadan poem are reproduced courtesy of http://submission.org; p.22 © The Islamic Foundation; p.106 © Ann Johnson (*The Guardian*). Every effort has been made to trace all copyright holders, but if any have been inadvertently overlooked the Publishers will be pleased to make the necessary arrangements at the first opportunity.

Although every effort has been made to ensure that website addresses are correct at time of going to press, Hodder Gibson cannot be held responsible for the content of any website mentioned in this book. It is sometimes possible to find a relocated web page by typing in the address of the home page for a website in the URL window of your browser.

Orders: please contact Bookpoint Ltd, 130 Milton Park, Abingdon, Oxon OX14 4SB. Telephone: (44) 01235 827720. Fax: (44) 01235 400454. Lines are open from 9.00–5.00, Monday to Saturday, with a 24-hour message answering service. Visit our website at www.hoddereducation.co.uk. Hodder Gibson can be contacted direct on: Tel: 0141 848 1609; Fax: 0141 889 6315; email: hoddergibson@hodder.co.uk

© Patricia Watson and Robert McVeigh 2006
First published in 2006 by
Hodder Gibson, a member of the Hodder Headline Group
2a Christie Street
Paisley PA1 1NB

Impression number   10 9 8 7 6 5 4 3 2 1
Year   2010 2009 2008 2007 2006

Cover photo Top row, second left and right: © Richard Olivier/ CORBIS; Second row, left: Photodisc Green/Getty Images, centre: © Tim Page/CORBIS; Third row, right: Corel Corporation; Fourth row, left: BrandXPictures/Getty Images, right: Cornstock/ Getty Images

Typeset in 12 on 14pt Giovanni by
Phoenix Photosetting, Chatham, Kent
Printed and bound in Italy.
Artwork by Mary Hall and Clive Spong (Linden Artists).

A catalogue record for this title is available from the British Library

ISBN-10: 0 340-88989-6
ISBN-13: 978-0-340-88989

Contents

Teacher's Notes

Personal Search

This series of books is aimed at P7–S2 pupils. The authors believe that 'personal search' lies at the heart of religious and moral education (RME) and is 'a process by which pupils can discover and develop their own beliefs and values.' (*Effective Teaching of Religious and Moral Education: Personal Search*, LT Scotland 2001) This definition is in keeping with the National Guidelines: Religious and Moral Education 5–14 which state that one of the aims of RME is for pupils to 'to develop their own beliefs, attitudes, moral values and practices through a process of personal search, discovery and critical evaluation.'

The study of religions

The authors believe that RME is essentially about the study of religions and this study has a significant role to play in personal search in developing pupils' beliefs and values. Although a pupil's beliefs and values develop in a number of ways both within and outside school, the study of religions provides a distinctive approach.

It is helpful to study religion through its central features. The National Guidelines identify five key features – celebrations, festivals, ceremonies and customs; sacred writings, stories and key figures; beliefs; sacred places, worship and symbols (practices); and moral values and attitudes. In these Personal Search books each religion is explored through units relating to these key features as set out below.

Each book covers two religions. Religions have been paired according to their dates of origins: Hinduism and Judaism are the earliest, then Buddhism and Christianity, and finally Islam and Sikhism.

Although there is no explicit study of non-religious systems of belief such as Humanism, there are opportunities to consider non-religious stances for living, as well as religious stances, on issues such as the

	Festivals and celebrations	Stories and key figures	Beliefs	Practices	Values
Buddhism	Ordination	The Buddha's teaching	Impermanence	Meditation	Karuna
Christianity	Easter	The Sermon on the Mount	Creation	Holy Communion	Agape
Hinduism	Samskaras	The Ramayana	Reincarnation	Puja	Dharma
Judaism	Yom Kippur	The story of Esther	Suffering	Kashrut	Tzedakah
Islam	Ramadan	Muhammad	Submission	Hajj	Ummah
Sikhism	The Khalsa	Guru Granth Sahib	Mool Mantra	The Langar	Vand Chhakna

origins of the universe, the existence of God, suffering and evil, relationships and moral values.

Stimulus material

Each unit contains stimulus material for pupils to engage with. This includes texts, stories, creedal statements, personal testimonies and experiences. The aim of the stimulus material is to involve pupils in dialogue with religions so that they can find out about the beliefs and values of religious believers in an atmosphere of enquiry, openness and critical discussion.

Teaching and learning

Each unit begins with a statement of the content to be covered and identifies the main concepts and themes. Personal search questions and activities focus on these concepts and themes. The units make use of a process to enhance personal search which was first introduced in *Effective Teaching of Religious and Moral Education: Personal Search* (LT Scotland 2001). This process has **three** stages:

- Finding out
- Making connections
- Thinking it over

Finding out
This involves finding out about the beliefs, values and practices of religious traditions. Pupils should be encouraged to appreciate the importance of knowledge and evidence as the basis for developing their own beliefs and values, and for justifying their own opinions.

Making connections
This involves connecting other people's beliefs, values and practices to pupils' own ideas and life experiences. Pupils' experiences of family, friendships and belonging to a community already shape their intellectual, social and moral development. This stage provides opportunities for pupils to reflect, talk about and share their own ideas and experiences.

Thinking it over
This involves creating opportunities for dialogue around the concepts and themes that emerge from the study of religions and pupils' own experience of life. Thinking it over should be challenging, dealing with issues that push children's thinking beyond the immediate knowledge of the content. The issues will invite discussion on a range of questions to do with God, suffering, evil, right and wrong, life and death, relationships, moral and social values, and the nature and origins of the natural world.

The three stages of the process need not take place in the order in which they are set out above. A unit may begin by finding out more about a religion, or perhaps by connecting with some aspect of pupil experience, or even by raising an issue for discussion. It is likely that discussion and activities will move backwards and forwards between each stage of the process.

Activities
Within the 'finding out' activities there are opportunities for further investigation and research. Pupils will need access to other resources including books, audio-visual materials and the Internet. In some of the 'making connections' and 'thinking it over' questions and activities teachers might encourage pupils to work together in small groups to discuss, share ideas and exchange views.

Choosing religions and units

There is no prescribed order in which religions or units within a religion should be studied. Schools might study one or more religions or select units from across religions using the key features.

Progression

The three books in this series provide materials for pupils throughout P7–S2. Pupils' maturity of thinking will develop over the three years, as will their reading, writing and interpretation skills. The units vary in terms of language level and difficulty of questions and tasks. Consequently, teachers should be selective with regard to these depending on pupils' age, stage and abilities. Attainment targets from the National Guidelines have not been included but teachers should use the Guidelines to ensure that pupils achieve their full potential.

Assessment

By looking at pupil responses to the various tasks, talking to individual pupils about their responses, and listening to pupils' discussion, teachers will be able to gather evidence about pupils' personal search skills. Pupils, through completing the activities in the books, should be able to state their views clearly on issues associated with the concepts identified at the beginning of each unit. They should be able to support these views with reasons and evidence in writing or in speech, and at some length. If pupils do this, they are demonstrating personal search skills.

Islam

 # Ramadan

Ramadan is the ninth month of the Muslim year during which Muslims all over the world fast. By fasting Muslims are obedient to Allah and try to improve their self-discipline and control.

stimulus 1

Parveen's letter to her Gran

IN THIS SECTION YOU WILL BE ASKED TO THINK ABOUT...

✓ Saum (fasting)

✓ Obedience

✓ Self-discipline

✓ Self-control

Dear Gran

Tomorrow is a big day for me. It's the start of Ramadan. For the first time I am going to fast for the whole month, not eating and drinking during the hours of daylight. Dad will be giving up smoking as well – he'll find that hard. I'll try to give up my bad habit of biting my nails. I had an argument with my best friend last week. Dad says that I must make it up with her. Part of doing the fast, he says, is thinking about being a better person and getting on well with people. I'm going round to see her tonight to see if we can make it up.

I'm a bit nervous about doing without food. I hope I'll be able to cope. The sun rises just before 6 o'clock so I'll get up about 5.30 and have something to eat before the fast begins. Mum says that it will have to be something to give me enough energy to keep me going through the day. At the end of the day she says it would be silly to stuff ourselves with food, so most days we'll break the fast with apricots which have been soaked in sugared water.

It is important to have a good breakfast before the daily fast during Ramadan

Ali is a bit peeved. He is only seven and not old enough to do the fast for a whole month, and he is making a fuss about it. He's going to do the fast at weekends. Aunt Nadira is pregnant so she is not doing the fast as well.

As you know there are many Muslims in our school and at lunchtime we'll be meeting together in a room in school to help each other get through the day. It's amazing to think that there will be millions of Muslims throughout the world fasting at this time. It really makes you realise you belong to a big community. Just thinking about that gives you a lot of strength and encouragement.

A Qur'an class

An Imam

After we have broken the fast each evening, we are going to get together as a family and read part of the Qur'an. At Qur'an class the other day, the Imam was telling us that we fast because it says in the Qur'an that it has been ordered by Allah. The Imam was also telling us that during Ramadan we should think of those who are hungry all the time, and not just in Ramadan. Some of my friends and I are going to organise a Bring and Buy Sale and raise money for Muslim Aid.

Mum says that you are coming to visit us after Ramadan to join us for our Eid-ul-Fitr celebrations. I'm looking forward to that. Our Imam says that Eid is a day of reward – and we will certainly deserve a reward after the fast. See you at the end of the month.

Love Parveen

1. Parveen and her father will not eat and drink during the hours of daylight during Ramadan.

   a) What will Parveen's father also try to give up?
   b) What will Parveen try to stop doing?
   c) Who do you think will find it easier – Parveen or her father? Why?

2. Why will Parveen try to improve relationships with her friend at the beginning of Ramadan?

3. Would Parveen find it easier to fast during winter or summer? Give a reason for your answer.

4. Who do you think will find the fast easier – a Muslim living in Scotland or a Muslim living in Egypt? Why?

5. a) Who is excused from the fast in Parveen's family?
   b) Why do you think they are excused?
   c) Look up books on Islam to find out who else is excused from the fast.
   d) Produce a chart showing who is excused and why.

6. a) What advice does Parveen's mum give about what she should eat before the fast begins in the morning?
   b) What food do you think might be good to eat at that time? Why?

7. a) How does Parveen's school help her and other Muslims during Ramadan?
   b) In what other ways do you think the school could help?

8. What is the celebration called at the end of Ramadan?

MAKING CONNECTIONS

1. Keep a record of your eating habits for five days. Include snacking. Other than when you were sleeping, what was the longest period of time you did without food?

2. Share experiences of times when you have done without food for quite a long period of time. Why did you do without food? How did you feel at the time? What did you miss most?

3. What things have you and members of your family tried to give up? Why did you want to give it up? Were you successful? Was it easy or hard?

stimulus
2

Teaching about fasting in the Qur'an

O you who believe, fasting is ordered for you as it was ordered for those before you. (Surah 2:183)

Those who can fast, but with great difficulty, may substitute feeding one poor person for each day of breaking the fast. (Surah 2:184)

Ramadan is the month during which the Qur'an was revealed, providing guidance for the people...Those who witness this month shall fast therein. (Surah 2:185)

One may eat and drink at any time during the night until you can plainly distinguish a white thread from a black thread by the daylight: then keep the fast until night. (Surah 2:187)

❶ What is the Qur'an?

❷ What reason is given in the first quotation for Muslims keeping the fast?

❸ Why was Ramadan chosen as the month of fasting?

❹ a) What might Muslims do if they find it difficult to fast?
   b) Give a reason why some Muslims might find it difficult to fast.

❺ How can pieces of thread be used to tell when night is over and day begins?

The benefits of fasting

Fasting has many benefits for the believer:

1 It makes the believer stronger as a believer, closer to God, and happier to be with God and to obey him.

2 It teaches the believer self-discipline because the person fasting controls his or her desire or need to drink and eat during the fasting period. People who learn self-control can resist wrongdoing or following their friends just to be like everyone else.

3 It gives believers a chance to feel what a hungry, needy person feels when he or she does not have enough food to eat. Believers can understand the importance of giving to charity and helping the hungry and needy people.

4 It is a healthy practice because it gives the body a chance to rest and get rid of some unwanted weight or materials in our body system.

5 Ramadan is the month of the revelation of the Qur'an and it is one of the best times of the year for the whole family to get together and study the Qur'an and learn more about their religion.

6 Fasting with the rest of believers in the world brings a feeling of unity and strength to all those fasting. Fasting together strengthens the whole family and makes them feel closer.

(www.submission.org)

1. Read each of the benefits of fasting carefully. Write down a heading for each one and explain it in your own words.

2. Look back at Parveen's letter (Stimulus 1). What benefits and reasons for fasting does she refer to in her letter? Write down the words she uses in her letter.

3. Imagine you are a youth worker, working with young people in a Mosque. It will soon be Ramadan. You have been asked to help the young people at the Mosque appreciate why it is good for Muslims to fast. You decide to produce a poster which shows one of the benefits of fasting for Muslims. In groups select one of the six benefits. Discuss what should be on the poster and what makes a good poster. Produce your poster.

MAKING CONNECTIONS

1. Look at the first benefit in the Stimulus. It is about Muslims being obedient to God and doing what God orders Muslims to do. What does it mean to be obedient? Who do you obey? Why?

2. Fasting helps Muslims to develop self-discipline. Explain how this headline illustrates a lack of self-discipline.

Victim of road-rage attack critically injured

3. Have you ever lost self-control? Briefly outline what happened.

4. Keeping your temper when provoked is an example of self-control. Identify times in your own life when you have shown self-discipline and control.

5. Which of the benefits is about keeping a healthy body? What do you do to try to keep your body healthy?

6. Look at benefit number 6. What do you think it means when it says fasting 'strengthens the whole family and makes them feel closer'? What does your family do to make its members feel close?

Thinking it over

❶ Look at the six benefits of fasting. Work in pairs and place the benefits in order of importance. Start with what you think is the most important and end with what you think is the least important. Compare your answers with another pair.

❷ Muslims believe that Ramadan helps them develop self-discipline. Do you think it is important to improve your self-discipline? Can you think of ways people could improve their self-discipline?

❸ What is meant by peer pressure? How is the scenario opposite an example of peer pressure? Give an example of peer pressure from your experience. Muslims would say that fasting could help with peer pressure. Why would they argue this? Do you agree?

❹ Muslims believe Ramadan helps them to think about what sort of person they are and how they can become a better person. Do you think everybody should think about how they might be a better person? If there was just one thing you would want to change about yourself what would it be? Why? How do you think you might change it?

 **stimulus**

4 Experiences of Ramadan

The first couple of days of Ramadan are hard whether you work in a restaurant like me or not. You're so used to being able to drink water, or even wee things like chewing gum, but after the third or fourth day you just fall into a routine. Some days you'll have a sore head, you'll be craving water, you'll feel weak but you can't break the fast because it's about not taking what you have for granted…

I've been doing Ramadan from a very young age, when my family moved to Scotland from Morocco. I guess you could say I'm a hypocrite because I usually go out dancing and drinking a lot, but for that one month I want to take a step back from my normal routine. It can be a bit difficult to fit in my daily prayers sometimes because I work in a restaurant that serves alcohol. It's not big enough for me to have my own wee room where I could go, wash, do my prayers and then go back to work. I usually have to wait until I get home and have a shower because it's important to be clean when you're praying…

I definitely feel good after Ramadan – I feel at ease and at peace. By the end I also feel physically stronger despite all the fasting. It's the one time of year that my whole family gets together: we eat together, we socialise together, we join others together for that one month.

Extracted from The Big Issue in Scotland, October 20–26, 2005

At times it isn't possible for me to fast given the kind of work I do. If I've got a long day in the operating theatre and I'm on my feet all day, it can be really tiring. Also I've got a tendency to faint if I don't have anything to eat. One year I had several colleagues who were interested in learning more about Ramadan. It was great because there were five Scottish people, a Hindu guy and a Chinese girl. We decided we'd all fast together for a day, then go out together in the evening for a meal. That's pretty much what Ramadan's about and it was nice of them to get a sense of what I was going through…

We had one guy who cheated and was finger-pointed by the rest of us in the group. I tried to explain that we don't just do it to feel hungry – we do it to try and remember those who are less fortunate and also for a bit of self-discipline and control…I think we sometimes need something to make us stop and think about life and Ramadan is a great time for reflection…We live in a western culture where the majority of people we live with aren't Muslim. But I think there are certain aspects we should always try to maintain.

Extracted from The Big Issue in Scotland, October 20–26, 2005

FINDING OUT

❶ Explain the practical difficulties the waitress has in keeping Ramadan at the restaurant.

❷ What difficulties does the doctor face in keeping Ramadan during his work at the hospital?

❸ How does the waitress change her lifestyle during Ramadan?

❹ Explain why the waitress thinks it important to keep Ramadan.

❺ Explain the reasons the doctor keeps Ramadan.

Thinking it over

❶ 'I definitely feel good after Ramadan – I feel at ease and peace' (the waitress). What does she mean? How do you think Ramadan helps her to feel at ease and peace? Do you think most people you know are at ease and peace? Why/why not? Is it important to feel at ease and peace? What do you think people can do to feel at ease and peace?

❷ Some of the doctor's non-Muslim friends joined him in the fast. Do you think this is a good idea? Do you think it is a good idea to share the experiences of another religion? Why/why not?

❸ 'We sometimes need something to make us stop and think about life and Ramadan is a great time for reflection' (the doctor). Why do you think the doctor says this? Do you agree everybody should stop and think about life? What is it about life that people should think about?

❹ Look at the last two sentences of the doctor's statement. What do you think he means? Do you think it is easy or difficult being a Muslim in a western society?

❺ 'It is considered to be very bad mannered to eat or drink or smoke in front of a Muslim who is fasting.' Why do you think this is? Do you agree?

5 Introducing Muslim children to Ramadan

Although young Muslims do not fast throughout the month of Ramadan, they are encouraged to think of Ramadan as an important and special time. So at this time young Muslims might sing songs, listen to poems and get involved in making and doing activities to help them learn about Ramadan.

Making a Ramadan Calendar Chain

- Cut coloured strips of paper into approximately 40cm lengths (30 strips are needed). Glue or staple them together into a chain.
- Make a Muslim pattern on each strip and alternate the colours of the rings.
- You will need 30 links (rings) in your chain – one for each day until the end of Ramadan. (Ramadan sometimes has 29 days not 30.)
- Hang your chain on a wall or in a doorway.
- Every day neatly tear off one of the rings until the end of Ramadan.

Ramadan song

Verse 1
Ramadan has come upon us
Ramadan God's holy month!
Praise be to Him for choosing us
To submit, to pray, to fast!

Chorus
Ramadan, Ramadan
Again is here,
Month of fast,
Ramadan, Ramadan
Truth is clear,
Faith will last.

Verse 2
I can feel the pangs of hunger
Which poor ones feel every day,
Oh my heart feels so much softer
I must help them in some way!

Chorus

Verse 3
Gratefulness I feel so strongly
Knowing tonight I will eat
While the poor ones will stay hungry
Even after the Sun has set.

Chorus

Verse 4
Discipline now I am learning
How to tell and to mean 'No!'
So if I meet an evil-monger
I will tell him where to go!

Chorus

(www.submission.org)

Ramadan poem

The holy month of Ramadan
For the Muslims [submitters] has begun
Praising God through the day,
From dawn to dusk we fast and pray.
We pay Zakat [charity] for those in need,
Trying our best to do good deeds.
When the Sun has set and day is done
I'll break the chain, but only one.
By the end of Ramadan, this whole chain will
Be all gone!
It's time to celebrate and share in the fun!

(www.submission.org)

Thinking it over

❶ 'Doing activities like the ones above strengthens family life.' Do you agree?

❷ Which of the above do you think a young Muslim would enjoy most? Why?

❸ Which of the above do you think will be the best for teaching young Muslims what Ramadan is about?

❹ Which of these statements do you agree with? Give reasons for you view

> Parents shouldn't involve their children in religion – they should wait until they are old enough to think about religion for themselves.

> It's really important that children learn about their religion.

Look at the song.

❶ Match a verse to a statement below:
  • Being thankful for having food to eat.
  • Feeling compassion for people who are hungry.
  • Praising God for giving the special month of Ramadan.
  • Remembering that Ramadan is about developing self-discipline.

❷ Write a short paragraph explaining what the song teaches young Muslims about Ramadan.

❸ Explain in your own words what young Muslims do with the Ramadan calendar chain once it is made.

❹ What does this activity teach young Muslims about Ramadan?

❺ Why does Ramadan sometimes last for 29 days and sometimes for 30 days?

❻ Use each of the following words in sentences to show what young Muslims might do during Ramadan: praising; paying; doing our best.

❼ How does the poem have a connection with making the Ramadan calendar chain?

stimulus

6 *Eid-ul-Fitr*

The fast of Ramadan ends with the Festival of Eid-ul-Fitr.

Sayings from the Hadith

When Eid-ul-Fitr arrives, the angels stand at the doorways and call upon Muslims: O company of Muslims, go to the generous God, who gave you the good things and grants the great reward. For God ordered you to pray during the night, so you prayed, ordered you to fast during the day, so you fasted and obeyed your Lord, so now take your reward.

A fasting person will have joy and happiness twice. When he breaks the fast he will be full of joy because it is at an end, and when he meets the Lord on the day of judgement, because he has kept his obligation

Muslims greeting each other after visiting the mosque at Eid

I always look forward to Eid – it's a great time. Usually I get some new clothes which I wear when we go to the Mosque in the morning for prayers. We meet other members of our family there and our friends and greet each other with the words 'Eid Mubarak'. After that we have a big family celebration. My grandparents, aunts and uncles and my cousins all get together – sometimes it's at our house and sometimes it's at one of my uncles'. This is a good time because my aunts and uncles give me presents – some give me money and all the children also get sweets. At the school I attend we have been making Eid cards so I always give out the cards I have made. The best part of the day is the family meal at lunch-time – lots of great food. I've not been fasting, well only a little bit, but everybody enjoys being able to eat in the daytime again. Then in the afternoon we visit as many of our friends as we can.

Nine-year-old Latifa explains why Eid-ul-Fitr is a happy day.

In our family we take Ramadan very seriously. All of us fast, apart from Latifa who is too young, though she does it at the weekend. So when Ramadan ends and the new moon signals the start of Shawaal, the next month, we are so pleased and happy. We are pleased that fasting is over and that we have been obedient and kept the fast. Eid is a good time for the children and it pleases me to see them so happy. They enjoy, as I do, meeting up with family and friends and celebrating together. For me the most important part of the day is when we go to the Mosque together to pray. I always say a quiet thank you for being given the strength to complete the fast. Our Imam always tells us in the talk he gives us that we have to think of others not as lucky as us, and he reminds us that we should have paid our zakat-ul-fitr – the charity of the fast – so that poor people can also enjoy the celebration. But most of all I am thankful for the good things Allah has given us.

Latifa's father explains why Eid-ul-Fitr is important to him.

Eid cards

❶ According to the first saying in the Hadith, Eid-ul-Fitr is a reward for Muslims. Why do Muslims deserve a reward?

❷ In the first saying God is described as generous. How does God, according to Muslims, show his generosity?

❸ According to the second saying why does a Muslim who has been fasting have joy and happiness twice?

❹ Explain in your own words why Eid is a happy day for Latifa.

❺ Explain in your own words why Eid is an important day for Latifa's father.

❻ What is the main difference between what Lafita thinks is important about Eid-ul-Fitr and what her father thinks is important?

Thinking it over

❶ The festival of Breaking the Fast often means more to Muslims living in western countries, such as Britain, than it does to those living in Eastern countries, such as Pakistan. Why do you think this is?

❷ Eid-ul-Fitr is described as 'a day of reward'. Is this a good description for the festival? Why/why not?

❸ 'Feasting is more important than fasting.' Why might someone say this? Do you think Muslims would agree with this?

❹ Explain what is meant in the second saying in the Hadith by the phrase 'when he meets the Lord on the day of judgement'. How might belief in a day of judgement affect how Muslims live their lives? Do you believe that one day people will be judged? Why/why not?

❺ Write a short paragraph about why you think Ramadan is important to Muslims and how it helps them in their daily life.

Muhammad

uhammad is a key figure in Islam. Muslims believe that Allah sent prophets to tell people about Allah. Muhammad, Muslims believe, is the last and final prophet.

stimulus 1 Muhammad's life

Muhammad lived from about 570CE to 632CE. He was born and lived much of his life in the town of Makkah, which today is in the country of Saudi Arabia.

IN THIS SECTION YOU WILL BE ASKED TO THINK ABOUT...

✓ Prophecy

✓ Revelation

✓ Muhammad as an exemplar and model for Muslims

✓ Leadership

✓ Shahadah

Mount Hira

My name is Abdullah. I live in Makkah and make good money working as a trader. I'd like to tell you about a man who has been causing a bit of a stir in the town in recent years. He's called Muhammad. Some people like him and listen to his teachings but he's made some enemies.

Muhammad had quite a hard life as a lad. His father died before he was born and then his mother died when he was quite young. First his grandfather looked after him, and when he died Muhammad went to live with an uncle. His uncle was a wealthy merchant so Muhammad did OK. When he grew up he worked for a while as a shepherd, and then became a businessman. He developed a good reputation as an honest person, who never cheated in his business dealings. In fact he was known as the trustworthy one and the truthful one. Everybody respected him. When he was about 25 he married a woman called Khadija, who was a bit older than him and they started a family.

Then when he was about 40 something happened which changed his life completely. It seems that he often visited a cave, outside the town, on Mount Hira to pray and think. One day he had some sort of religious experience. He was praying when he saw an angel, the angel Jibrel, who spoke to him. Muhammad said the angel revealed a special message from Allah for the people of Makkah. This message was that the people of Makkah should stop worshipping statues of gods, and worship the one true God, Allah. Over the next few years Muhammad received many such messages about how Allah wanted the people to live their lives, and how Allah would judge them one day.

The word 'angel' means a messenger and the angel revealed to Muhammad teachings about Allah. These revelations were at first memorised, and then written down. Eventually, after Muhammad's death, they were collected together in one Book. This is the Qur'an, the Muslim Holy Book.

Muslims call the journey Muhammad made from Makkah to Madinah the Hijrah. The year Muhammad made this journey is important in Islam. It is the year from which Muslims date their calendar. Later, in about 630CE, Muhammad returned to Makkah. Two years later he died and his tomb is in Madinah.

Over the next few years Muhammad began to tell people about these revelations he had received from Allah. At first he told only his family and a few friends, but eventually he started preaching to the people of Makkah. There's only one God, he preached. Stop worshipping your idols; destroy them; change your ways; you are not following Allah's teaching; Allah will judge you one day.

Some people followed his teachings, but he made many enemies and some of his followers were persecuted. He particularly upset my wife. She had, in our house, a number of statues of gods, which she worshipped every day. Muhammad said this was wrong and foolish. He told her the statues are just stone, they are useless, they can't do anything. Submit to the will of Allah, the one true God. Well, in recent months things have come to a head. It's about 12 years since his first revelation and some people have had enough of Muhammad. They are making life difficult for him and his followers. So the latest news is he's moved on. He's left Makkah. Rumour has it that he has gone to a town to the north of Makkah called Madinah. The leaders there have invited him to help build a community based on his teachings. Many in Makkah are pleased he's gone. I'm not so sure. He seemed a good man to me, and I think there was something in what he was saying.

The Prophet's mosque in Madinah

1 Look at the following statements about Muhammad's life and place them in the correct sequence:
- Muhammad's mother died.
- Muhammad received his first revelation.
- Muhammad left Makkah for Madinah.
- Muhammad was born.
- Muhammad became a businessman.
- Muhammad died.
- Muhammad returned to Makkah.
- Muhammad got married.
- Muhammad preached in Makkah.
- Muhammad's uncle looked after him.

2 Muhammad was born about 570CE. Work out the year he was married; the year he received his first revelation; the year he left Makkah for Madinah.

3 Work in small groups. Research one of the following aspects of Muhammad's life:
- His birth and early life up to and including his marriage.
- The details of how he received his first revelation from the angel Jibrel on Mount Hira.
- The time he left Makkah and spent in Madinah.
- His successful return to Makkah.

4 Write in your own words the main points of Muhammad's message to the people of Makkah.

5 Design a placard which summarises Muhammad's message.

6 A keyword in the story of Muhammad is 'revelation'. Look it up in a dictionary and discuss in class what it means. Write down in your own words why it is an important word in the story of Muhammad.

stimulus 2 *Sayings of Muhammad*

As well as the revelations given by angel Jibrel, there are other sayings of Muhammad. These are found in the Hadith, a collection of Muhammad's sayings and actions.

1 None of you is a true believer until he wishes for his brother what he wishes for himself.

2 He is not a believer who eats his fill while his neighbour is hungry.

3 Whoever of you sees an evil action, let him change it with his hand, and if he is not able to do so, then with his tongue, and if he is not able to do so, then with his heart – and that is the weakest of faith.

4 He who has no compassion for our little ones, and does not acknowledge the honour due to our elders, is not one of us.

5 No one has eaten better food than what he earns with the toil of his own hands.

6 The earth is green and beautiful and Allah has appointed you his steward over it.

7 Each person's joint must perform a charity every day the sun comes up: to act justly between two people is a charity; to help a man with his mount, lifting him on to it or hoisting up his belongings on to it is a charity; a good word is a charity; every step you take to prayers is a charity; and removing a harmful thing from the road is a charity.

FINDING OUT

❶ What is the Hadith?

❷ Look at sayings 1–6 and the slogans below. Match a saying to each of the slogans.

❸ Look at the saying number 7. What is meant by charity in this saying?

❹ The saying identifies different things which are acts of charity. Write down each one in you own words.

❺ What do all these sayings teach about the sort of person a Muslim should be?

Thinking it over

❶ Look at sayings 1–6 and the slogans. For each, think of an example explaining why the saying is appropriate for today's world.

❷ Which saying do you think is most relevant for today's world? Which saying do you think is least relevant for today's world? Give reasons for your answers.

❸ Identify in your own words the three different ways of responding to an evil action. Why do you think the last way is seen as the weakest way?

❹ Saying 7, about charity, is well over 1300 years old. Which parts of it do you think are relevant for today's world and which parts are not so relevant? Rewrite the saying for today's world.

A woman was slowly walking through the city of Makkah. She was laden down with bags and bundles. She looked tired, worn out and sad as she struggled along the road. A man called out to her, 'Where are you going, can I help you?'

'Oh please sir,' she replied, 'I'd be very grateful if you could help. But I'm going to the next town, and that's quite a way – you won't want to go that far.'

'That's OK' he replied as he took the bags and bundles from her, 'but tell me why are you leaving Makkah, and it looks to me as if you are taking all your possessions with you. Are you leaving for good?'

'Yes' she replied 'I'm fed up living here. This used to be a good town to live in but now it isn't. This man Muhammad is causing all sorts of trouble. He goes round preaching and upsetting everybody. So I'm leaving for good. If only people were like you, sir, then Makkah would be a good place to live. Tell me sir, who are you – I don't think we have met before – what is your name?'

'My name is Muhammad' the man replied, 'and I worship the one true God, Allah.'

'In that case' said the woman, 'I'm staying – please take me home – I want to follow your teaching.'

 **stimulus 3**

A story about Muhammad

Muhammad taught by example as well as by words. This story took place when Muhammad was living in Makkah and was unpopular because of the message he preached.

  **FINDING OUT**

❶ Why did the woman say she wanted to leave Makkah?

❷ Why did she decide to stay?

❸ What does this story teach about what sort of person Muhammad was?

MAKING CONNECTIONS

❶ 'Muhammad taught by example as well as words.' What does this mean? Who has been a good example for you to follow? Why were they a good example? What did you learn from their example?

❷ A well-known saying is 'actions speak louder than words'. What does it mean? How does it apply to the story about Muhammad? Work in small groups to produce a short drama which illustrates the saying.

❸ Are you expected to be a good example to someone, such as a younger brother or sister? Is it fair that you are expected to be a good example? Is it easy or hard to be a good example?

❹ Muhammad practised what he preached. Do people always practise what they preach? Use a dictionary to find out what the word 'hypocrite' means. Can you think of a time when someone has been a hypocrite?

❺ Write a short story which illustrates the saying 'practise what you preach'.

stimulus **4**

The Shahadah

The Shahadah can be seen on the flag of Saudi Arabia

There is no God but Allah and Muhammad is his Prophet.

Facts about the Shahadah:

1 The Shahadah is the first of the five Pillars of Islam.
2 The Shahadah is a statement of Muslim belief.
3 The Shahadah has two parts to it.
  First, it teaches the main belief of Islam which was revealed to Muhammad that there is only one God. This belief is called 'monotheism'. Mono means one and theism means 'God'.
  Second, it explains the importance of Muhammad in Islam as the prophet of God.
4 Muhammad is regarded as the last and final prophet. There have been many prophets but Muhammad, Muslims believe, is the last.

5 Muhammad is called the Seal of the Prophets. A letter sealed with wax cannot be tampered with or altered. So Muhammad's message is the final message – it cannot be altered in any way.
6 Since Muhammad is the final prophet of Allah, he is respected. When muslims speak or write his name they add the phrase 'peace be upon him' (often abbreviated to PBUH) as a sign of respect.
7 The Shahadah is perhaps one of the most frequently spoken sentences in the world. It is said and listened to by millions of Muslims every day when they listen to the call to prayer and when they pray.
8 A person becomes a Muslim by repeating the Shahadah aloud publicly and with intent.

9   The first words a baby born into a Muslim family hears is the Shahadah.

❶ What are the two parts of the Shahadah?

❷ A dictionary has two meanings for the word 'prophet':
i) 'a person who foretells the future'
ii) 'a person inspired and chosen by God with a message for the people'.
Which definition relates to Muhammad? Why?

❸ Look at books about Islam and search the Internet to find out the names of some of the other prophets of Islam.

❹ Why is Muhammad regarded as the Seal of the Prophets?

❺ Explain why 'the Shahadah is one of the most frequently spoken sentences in the world'.

❻ How do Muslims show respect to Muhammad when writing or saying his name?

❼ The Shahadah is the first of the five Pillars of Faith. Find out what the other four Pillars are. What is the purpose of a pillar? Why is the 'five Pillars' a good title for the five Muslim practices?

The Five Pillars of Islam

MAKING CONNECTIONS

1 Muhammad was chosen by Allah to be his prophet. Have you ever been chosen to do something special? How did you feel? Were all your feelings positive or did you have some negative feelings? Were you glad you were chosen? Did you make a success of what you were chosen to do?

2 Is there anything you would especially like to be chosen to do? What is it? Why would you like to do it? Do you think you have the skills to do it?

3 Muslims show respect to Muhammad. Choose someone you respect who is no longer alive. Why do you respect that person?

4 Imagine you have to choose a leader for your class in school. What are the things you might take into account when making your choice?

Thinking it over

1 Do you think the world today needs a prophet? What do you think the prophet's message should be? Write your message in an imaginative way and contribute to a wall display headed 'Messages for Today's World'.

2 Is it a good idea to have a statement of belief which you say everyday? Why/why not? What would your statement of belief be?

3 Muslims respect Muhammad because he was a great leader and prophet for Muslims. Should religious and political leaders today always be respected? Why/why not?

stimulus 5

Muhammad – a model character for all Muslims

In God's messenger you have a model for someone who looks forward to meeting God at the Last Day and who mentions God frequently. (Surah 33:21)

During his lifetime, Muhammad (PBUH) demonstrated a noble and exemplary character. He was an absolute believer in one God, and was thoroughly trustworthy in respect of his companionship, help and guidance.

He was affectionate, kind and sympathetic to his compatriots: always considerate, truthful and sincere, perfectly faithful in respect of all trusts and promises.

He kept himself aloof from gambling, drinking, vulgar wrangling and all the vices that were rampant among the people of his time.

He was fair and honest in his dealings; generous and obliging to his friends and benefactors. The Prophet's life, therefore, became the model and perfect example for all Muslims, and for all times to come. To follow his traditions along with the guidance of the Qur'an is every true Muslim's earnest ambition.

(*RE Briefs on Islam: A Guide for Teachers*, The Islamic Foundation)

Muslim Poem

He was honest, truthful and very kind
And the greatest teacher of mankind
Who was exalted in his character too
And never strayed from what is true
Despite the obstacles that prevailed
He struggled on and never failed.

And Muhammad is his blessed name
Who called the **Tawhid** when he came
And in the process suffered much
But never lost his special touch
Of being polite and kind and good
And always called for brotherhood.

To everyone he brought much joy
Though he was orphaned as a boy
He always led a truthful life
Despite the hardship and the strife
For he was steadfast all the way
Submitting to Allah everyday.

He brought guidance so complete
And taught us how to pray and eat
While in the **Sunnah** you'll recall
Are detailed teachings for us all
And no more Prophets there will be
For he's the final one, you see.

(*Muslim Poems for Children* by Mymona Hendricks, The Islamic Foundation)

Tawhid is the Muslim belief in one God. Sunnah is a collection of Muhammad's sayings and conduct.

FINDING OUT

❶ How do you know the verse from Surah 33:21 of the Qur'an is about Muhammad?

❷ According to the verse from the Qur'an, who is Muhammad a model for?

❸ Using the extract about Muhammad:
- identify Muhammad's beliefs.
- identify words which describe Muhammad's character.
- identify the things which Muhammad avoided doing.
- identify what Muslims try to do.

❹ Look at each verse of the poem. Write a sentence to explain what each verse teaches about Muhammad.

❺ In your own words sum up what Muhammad was like as a person and why he is important to Muslims.

❻ Write your own short poem about Muhammad.

Thinking it over

❶ Some of the words used to describe Muhammad's qualities are: 'trustworthy; affectionate; kind; sympathetic; truthful; sincere; honest; generous. Muhammad was a religious leader. Which qualities do you think made Muhammad a great religious leader? Why?

❷ 'It is difficult for a Muslim in today's world to follow the example of Muhammad' Do you agree with this statement? Give reasons for your answer.

❸ What do you think non-Muslims can learn from the way Muhammad lived his life?

❹ 'Everybody needs a model to follow. The trouble today is that there are few good models, especially for young people.' Do you agree? What sort of person would make a good model for today?

 # Submission

The word Islam means 'submission' and a Muslim is someone who submits to the will of Allah. Submission means complete obedience to Allah. Muslims believe that they know what Allah wants because His message has been given directly to them and is held in the Qur'an. The Qur'an is a complete instruction book for life and Islam teaches that those who follow its teachings will be rewarded with an afterlife in Paradise. Those who do not submit to the will of Allah will be punished in the afterlife. To be a Muslim then, a person must be willing to accept that Allah has complete authority over his or her entire life including things like dress, diet and spending time every day in prayer.

IN THIS SECTION YOU WILL BE ASKED TO THINK ABOUT...

✓ Submission
✓ Obedience
✓ Devotion to God
✓ Authority

 **stimulus 1** ## Submission through prayer

Muslims show their continual submission to Allah through daily prayer. Muslims are expected to pray five times every day unless they have a very good reason for not doing so. This regular prayer shows that they are never too busy to give a bit of their time to worshipping Him.

Here are some important aspects of prayer in Islam:

Salah – prayer five times daily
Wudu – washing before prayer. There is a set routine for doing this

Rakahs – a set of different prayer positions
Quiblah – the position to face when praying. Muslims must find the direction of the Ka'aba in Makkah
Adhan – the call to prayer
Sutrah – any object which is placed in front so no one has to walk directly in front of the person praying. Anyone needing to pass in front of a Muslim praying should walk behind the sutrah.
Tayammum – when no water is available, Muslims touch earth with both hands and wipe it over the face and backs of the hands.

The seven prayer positions in Islam

The Adhan (Call to Prayer)

Allah is the Greatest (repeated four times).
I bear witness that nothing deserves to be worshipped except Allah (repeated twice).
I bear witness that Muhammad is the Messenger of Allah (repeated twice).
Come to prayer (repeated twice, turning the face to the right).
Come to success (repeated twice, turning the face to the left).
Allah is the Greatest (repeated twice).
Nothing deserves to be worshipped except Allah.

A Muezzin issuing the call to prayer

If you log on to www.islamicity.com/ PrayerTimes you can type in the name of your city and find the exact prayer times for today!

FINDING OUT

❶ Copy this word search puzzle into your jotter and circle the seven keywords hidden in it.

Then put them into alphabetical order with the meanings next to them in your jotter.

```
S U R Q C H A O L
Q U I B A A Q B A
H A L R S K U S H
W B T T H A I U Q
L U A U S R B O U
S K D T S U L M I
H R H U I S A K B
A Q A Y A D H A N
K T M L U T L A B
A K A R T S A R R
R H U A K A M T S
M U M M A Y A T A
```

❷ Make a poster of Muslim prayer rules. Include rules about the following: how often to pray, where to face while praying, how to prepare for prayer, what to do if no water is available.

❸ Read the call to prayer. Write down two phrases which illustrate the Muslim belief in submission to Allah.

❹ Why do Muslims believe that 'Nothing deserves to be worshipped except Allah'?

❺ Look carefully at the pictures of the Muslim girl praying. How does she show that 'Allah is the Greatest'? Draw the two prayer positions which you think best illustrate the idea of submission. Write a sentence to explain why you think each picture is a good example of submission.

❻ Find out more about the Muslim prayer rituals. What special objects do they use? What times of day do they pray? How do they know when it is time to pray? Use your information to produce a poster about 'Muslim Prayer'.

MAKING CONNECTIONS

❶ How are people usually expected to behave when they meet a king or a queen? Describe some other actions used to show that certain people are very important. In what ways is this similar to the Muslim prayer rituals? What do these actions tell us about the Muslim view of Allah?

❷ The Adhan is like a signal for Muslims to stop what they are doing and take time to pray. What signals might be used at the following times?
• Stop sleeping and get up for school.
• Change lessons.
• Half-time at a football match.
• Soldiers needing to fall into line.
• Time to go to church.
Can you think of more signals used in our society? What is the purpose of a signal? In what ways are these signals the same or different from the Adhan? Are they more or less important?

❸ Muslims often say that the time spent praying refreshes them for the next part of the day. How do you refresh yourself in the middle of a busy day? Make a list of suggestions for people who are not Muslim. How important do you think it is to take time out?

❹ Salah is a way of demonstrating commitment to Allah. What does commitment mean for you? How do you show commitment to:
a) your family?
b) your friends?
c) your school?
d) any organisations you are a member of?
e) God?

Thinking it over

1 What things might make it difficult for Muslims in Britain to pray five times a day? What can schools and employers do to help Muslims with this aspect of their lives? Should normal rules at school or work be changed for people with religious beliefs?

2 'People who believe in God believe prayer is a way to communicate with God.' How might praying to God help some people? What sorts of things do people pray to God for? Why do many people find it difficult to pray?

stimulus
2 *Submission through diet*

Dear Sarah

Thanks for your letter. I am glad that you are able to come and stay for a week during the summer holidays, it will give us a chance to really get to know each other. Being pen pals is great but I am very excited about actually meeting you.

One of the things I should perhaps warn you about is the food we eat. I hope you don't mind fruit and vegetables because we eat a lot of them. You see, we have some very strict rules about food although we can eat most things we would like to. Things which are allowed are called Halal and things which are not allowed are called Haram. Anything we are not sure about is called Mushbooh and should be avoided anyway. Dad says that it's important for us to keep these laws if we want to stay holy and have our prayers heard by Allah.

You don't need to worry too much about any of this though – there really is a good selection of things available. My mum and my gran are both great cooks and one of their specialities is home-made pizza which I am sure you will love! Since she moved to the UK my gran has had great fun trying out new recipes, although she sometimes finds it difficult to get Halal ingredients in our local supermarket. Often when I go shopping with her it's my job to read the labels of the things she wants to buy – her eyesight isn't what it used to be! I will ask her to cook you some traditional Pakistani dishes too. You'll find it much better than the stuff you get in your local Indian takeaway I can assure you.

Anyway that's enough on that just now. Mum said while you are here I can go shopping for new clothes, hopefully you can help me pick some things out. I need new jeans and tops for the holidays. We can also go to the cinema. I can't wait to meet you! Having you here will be like a holiday for me too!

Write soon

Love

Rasmia

O mankind! Eat of that which is lawful and wholesome in the earth, and follow not the footsteps of the devil. Lo! he is an open enemy for you. (Surah 2:168)

Eat of that which Allah hath bestowed on you as food lawful and good, and keep your duty to Allah in Whom ye are believers. (Surah 5:88)

Muslim Food Laws

Halal   *Haram*   *Mushbooh*

Halal	*Haram*	*Mushbooh*
Things which are allowed. Most things are Halal unless they are obviously either Haram or Mushbooh	*Foods which are strictly forbidden because they are considered unhealthy or dangerous for the mind. These include: alcohol; pork; lard; animals that were not slaughtered properly or which have died of a disease or were poisoned; animals which eat meat; birds of prey; blood or any product made with blood.*	*This category contains any foods which we are unsure about. If they might contain some ingredients from a forbidden source then we cannot eat them. Sometimes manufacturers don't provide every detail so if we have any doubts we shouldn't eat it! This might include things which have traces of alcohol or animal fat or flavourings*

Meat which is considered as Halal is slaughtered in the traditional way. The animals are killed quickly with a sharp knife while the name of Allah is said. This means that the animal's death is quick and there is no unnecessary pain. Animals which have died before they can be slaughtered are Haram because they may have been contaminated by disease or poison. This meat would not be healthy. Refusing to buy this meat means that the owners are encouraged to take care of their livestock to ensure the animals remain healthy. The Muslim Food Board has the job of certifying all foods as Halal, Haram or Mushbooh. This is an ongoing task because of the huge variety of new products brought out all the time.

FINDING OUT

1 Decide whether the following statements are true or false. Write the ones which are true into your jotter.
a) Muslims can eat anything they like.
b) Muslims only eat food which is Halal.
c) Only traditional Pakistani or Indian food is Halal.
d) Muslims are allowed to drink alcohol.
e) Sticking to Halal food is part of a Muslim's duty to Allah.
f) Muslims should not eat foods if they do not know what they contain.
g) Muslims can't shop at supermarkets like Asda, Tesco or Sainsburys.

2 Make up a menu for a Halal meal. The website www.eat-halal.com will give you some recipe ideas if you need help to get started.

3 What does the Muslim Food Board do? Why is this a difficult task?

4 Make a classroom wall display about Muslim food laws. Look through magazines and cut out pictures of different foods to illustrate Halal, Haram and Mushbooh.

5 Why is it sometimes difficult for Muslims in Britain to find Halal food?

6 Write a letter to the manager of a local supermarket. Find out if they make an effort to stock Halal foods or choose one of your favourite fast-food chains, write to them and find out if their foods would be Halal or Haram.

MAKING CONNECTIONS

1 Do you think the food you eat is healthy? Write down a list of the things you have eaten this week. Discuss your list with a partner and decide whether there are some things you should try to eat less of. Why is it important to eat healthy food?

2 Muslims are not the only people with special dietary laws. Do you know anyone who has a special diet? Apart from religion, for what other reasons might someone be on a special diet? How easy or difficult is it to eat out in Britain if you have special dietary rules to keep?

3 Keeping the dietary laws is a personal commitment for adult Muslims. If they break the laws deliberately they must wrestle with their own conscience since they alone must answer to Allah. What does it mean to wrestle with your conscience? Have you ever felt guilty about not sticking to something you know you should have?

Thinking it over

1 The Qur'an teaches that alcohol is bad for society. Do you agree or disagree? Should sales of alcohol be stricter in this country? Give reasons for your opinion.

2 Is it right that a religion should influence the food people eat? Do you think food manufacturers care enough about people with special diets? Should people have to pay more for food prepared according to religious laws?

3 Most animals in the UK are not slaughtered in the Muslim way. Find out how they are killed. Write arguments for and against both methods.

stimulus 3 *Submission through dress*

And say to the believing women that they should lower their gaze and guard their modesty; that they should not display their beauty and ornaments except what must ordinarily appear thereof; that they should draw their veils over their bosoms and not display their beauty except to their husbands, their fathers, their husband's fathers, their sons, ... (Surah 24: 31)

The Qur'an tells Muslims that they should dress modestly. Neither men nor women should go around showing off their bodies. In some Muslim countries women cover their whole body, even the face, but in other places they cover the head and the rest of the body but not the face. The key thing for women is that the clothes they wear should not attract unwanted attention from men.

Four Principles of Muslim Dress Code

1) Make sure the body is properly covered. For men this means from the navel to the knees. For women it means the whole body except the hands and face. Don't wear clothes which are tight fitting or see-through.

2) Clothes should look nice on the person. They should make both men and women look respectable. Generally men should try to keep most of their bodies covered so as not to offend anyone.

3) People should be able to tell you are a Muslim from the clothes you wear. This is something to be proud of.

4) Clothes should not be too fancy. In choosing clothes a Muslim must avoid showing off or trying to look better than others.

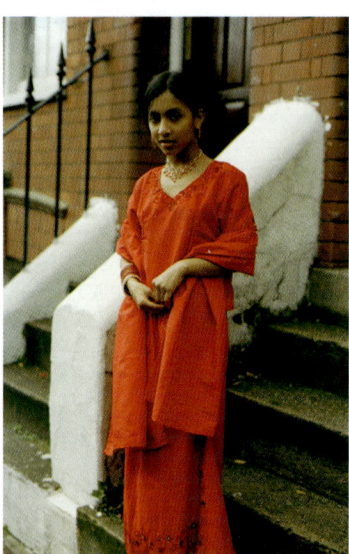

A Muslim girl wearing shalwar (trousers) and kameez (tunic)

Muslim women wearing the hijab

A Muslim man in traditional dress

FINDING OUT

1 What do you think the following phrases from the Qur'an mean?
  a) They should lower their gaze and guard their modesty.
  b) Except what must ordinarily appear thereof.
  c) Draw their veils over their bosoms and not display their beauty.

2 How have women from different Muslim countries put this teaching into practice?

3 Design a suitable traditional outfit for a Muslim man or woman. It can be for a special occasion or for everyday wear.

4 Muslim women living in Scotland often dress in the traditional Muslim way. Suggest two reasons why they don't want to wear western style clothes.

5 What advantages might there be for Muslim men and women if they follow the Muslim dress code?

6 How does the Muslim dress code show submission to Allah?

7 Aisha is a Muslim girl who wears the shalwar and kameez to school. She also covers her head with a scarf whenever she is in public. Imagine you are Aisha and write an article for your school magazine explaining why you wear the clothes you do.

8 Look through some clothes catalogues and cut out pictures of some clothes which Muslims might find offensive. Stick these in your jotter and write a paragraph explaining why Muslims would not want to wear these clothes.

MAKING CONNECTIONS

1 You can tell a lot about a person by the clothes they wear. What do the following clothes say about the person wearing them?

2 Who decides what clothes you wear to school and outside of school? Do you think people should have guidelines on what to wear at school, at work, or for sports? In what ways can it help if there are clear guidelines about what to wear? What can happen when people don't wear the correct clothes?

3 What clothes do you think are appropriate for the following occasions?
  a) Going to a wedding.
  b) Going to a funeral.
  c) Representing your school at a pupil conference.
  d) Going to a friend's birthday party.
  e) Going for a job interview.
  f) Lounging about at home.

4 Clothes can help to establish your identity. They can communicate something about your personality to others. What does your dress style say about your personality? Discuss how some people use clothes to present a certain image.

Thinking it over

❶

Hijab banned in schools

Discuss this headline. Do you think it is fair that Muslim girls are sometimes told not to wear the hijab in school? Why is it important to Muslim girls that they be allowed to wear this special headdress at school? How might the girls feel about going to school without their heads covered? What should Muslim parents do? What reasons might Head Teachers give for banning religious clothing in their school? Do you think the government should do anything about this situation?

❷

> It doesn't matter what you wear – what's important is your character and how you live.

> What you wear is important – it shows what sort of person you are.

Which statement do you agree with most? Why?

❸ Sometimes you just have to do as you are told without question, even if you disagree with what you are told to do.' Do you agree? Identify some situations when it is important to follow rules without question.

stimulus 4 A Muslim's relationship with Allah

Allah is beyond the limits of our world. He is the creator and since He created it He cannot be bound by it. He is all-seeing, all-knowing and the most powerful. Only Allah can truly know what is best for humans. We should follow His will and trust his Judgement. If we devote our lives to serving Him then the rewards will be great.

Human beings by their very nature are restricted in what they can do. They are limited by their human bodies and minds. They cannot see into the future nor truly understand the past. It is not then for humans to judge what is best for the planet, for society and for the future of universe.

In the name of Allah, Most Gracious, Most Merciful. Praise be to Allah, the Cherisher and Sustainer of the worlds; Most Gracious, Most Merciful; Master of the Day of Judgement. Thee do we worship, and Thine aid we seek. Show us the straight way, the way of those on whom Thou hast bestowed Thy Grace, those whose portion is not wrath, and who go not astray. (Surah 1:1–7)

Allah. There is no God but He, the Living, the Self-subsisting, Eternal. No slumber can seize Him nor sleep. His are all things in the heavens and on earth. Who is there can intercede in His presence except as He permitteth? He knoweth what appeareth to His creatures as before or after or behind them. Nor shall they compass aught of His knowledge except as He willeth. His Throne doth extend over the heavens and the earth, and He feeleth no fatigue in guarding and preserving them for He is the Most High, the Supreme (in glory). (Surah 2:255)

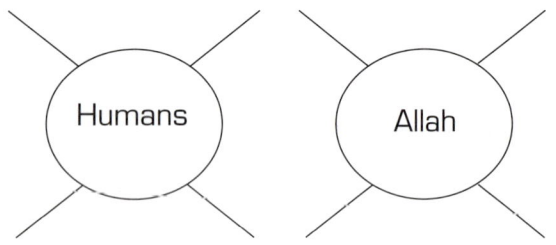

❶ Copy and complete the two spider diagrams to show how the difference between humans and Allah is described in Stimulus 4. Add as many legs to each spider as you can:

Humans

Allah

❷ Muslims actually have 99 different names for Allah. See if you can find out more of them and make up a wordsearch puzzle for someone else in your class to try.

❸ Work in groups. Each group should choose one of the names for Allah, explain what it means and what it teaches about Muslim belief about the nature of Allah.

❹ What do you think is meant by the term 'the straight way' in Surah 1:1–7?

❺ Use the information in Stimulus 4 to write a paragraph about 'The relationship between a Muslim and Allah'.

❻ Copy the table below and draw connecting lines to match up the statements from the Qur'an with the correct meaning.

Statements from the Qur'an	Meaning of statements
Thine Aid we seek.	He never gets tired of looking after them.
The Cherisher and Sustainer of the world.	He is always awake.
Those on whom Thy hast bestowed Thou Grace.	He needs nothing outside of Himself.
The Self-subsisting.	They'll only know what He wants them to know.
No slumber can sieze Him nor sleep.	Humans want Allah's help.
He knoweth what appeareth to His creatures.	The One who looks after us and cares for the world.
Nor shall they compass aught of his Knowledge except as He willeth.	He knows everything about us.
He feeleth no fatigue in guarding and preserving them.	Those people You have blessed.

Thinking it over

❶ What does it mean in the sport of wrestling when one wrestler submits to another? What does it mean when Muslims say 'we submit to the will of Allah'? Why is it necessary for Muslims to submit to the will of Allah?

❷ For Muslims, belief in Allah affects everything they do – what they eat, how they dress, how they spend their time. Do you think religious belief should have such an impact on how people live their lives? Give reasons for your answer. What are the things which help you decide how you live your life?

❸ Make a display for your classroom wall. Using large sheets of paper, draw two paths: one straight and one that twists and turns. Write words along each path to show the kinds of behaviour which might be considered 'straight' and the kinds of behaviour you might consider to be a bit 'twisty'. Discuss your ideas and see if you agree with each other about what is right and wrong behaviour.

❹ Allah is described as 'The Cherisher and Sustainer of the World'. Do you think humans are equipped well enough to judge what is best for the planet or do you think there is a higher authority like Allah who knows more than humans do? Give reasons for your answer.

Hajj

Hajj is one of the Five Pillars of Islam. Every Muslim who is healthy and wealthy enough is expected to complete the pilgrimage to Makkah at least once in a lifetime. During the time spent there, many rituals are performed which remind the pilgrims of events in the life of Prophet Muhammad. It is not an easy pilgrimage to make and not all Muslims are able to complete it. However, for those who do, it is the journey and experience of a lifetime. Hajj brings together Muslims from all parts of the world and helps to strengthen both the faith of the individual and the Muslim community as a whole.

IN THIS SECTION YOU WILL BE ASKED TO THINK ABOUT...

✓ Pilgrimage
✓ Rituals
✓ Faith
✓ Challenge
✓ Following rules

stimulus 1

The importance of the Ka'aba

The Ka'aba is important to me because I built it! It was the very first building intended for the worship of the one God. Well actually it was originally built by Adam, the first man on earth, but by the time I came along it had been totally destroyed. As a prophet of God on earth it was my job to stop people from worshipping idols. It was hard work rebuilding the Ka'aba in the middle of the Arabian desert but well worth all the effort when you consider how its importance has grown since then. Millions of people from all over the world visit it every year during Hajj.

Abraham

The Ka'aba is important to me because it is in the city of my birth, Makkah. I was Muhammad's uncle and I raised him as my own child after his parents had both died. During my lifetime the leaders of Makkah used the Ka'aba as a place of idol worship. When Muhammad tried to stop this, he and his followers were forced to flee Makkah and lived most of their lives in Madinah. I wish I could experience the thrill of visiting the Ka'aba today; it plays such a central role in our faith. I am proud of Muhammad though. He fought hard for many years to get the Ka'aba back and destroy those wretched statues.

Abu Talib

I was there the day that Muhammad marched with 10,000 supporters and regained control of the city of Makkah. It was the most exciting day of my life. Muhammad was so cool, calm and collected. The people of Makkah had no choice but to surrender, there were too many of us and too few of them. He ordered that there be no bloodshed in the holy city and he himself declared that those who had wronged us previously were to be forgiven. It was the most peaceful defeat of any city I've been involved in! Most people couldn't believe their ears at the time but it was just the kind of man he was. He didn't want lots of death and destruction, there had been plenty of that for years since we fled to Madinah. He just wanted to be able to worship at the holy shrine and to rid Makkah of the idols once and for all. On entering the city he rode his horse straight to the Ka'aba and circled it seven times. Early the next morning, he ordered the doors to be opened and brought out only two images which he chose to keep; a holy icon of the Virgin Mary holding the young child Jesus and an old painting of Abraham. He ordered his brother-in-law Othman to destroy everything else.

Abu Bakr

FINDING OUT

❶ Create a fact-file about the Ka'aba. Draw a picture and include information about who built it, where it is and explain why millions of Muslims visit it every year.

❷ Abu Talib mentions 'idol worship'. What is an idol?

❸ What does Abu Bakr's account teach us about Muhammad's personality?

❹ Try to imagine the scene when Muhammad circled the Ka'aba with 10,000 Muslims behind him. Explain how you think the following people would have felt:
a) Muhammad
b) His followers
c) The leaders of Makkah.

❺ Which images does Abu Bakr claim that Muhammad kept? Suggest some reasons to explain why he might have done this. What does this tell us about Islam and its response to other faiths?

❻ If mobile phones had existed at that time, how would an ordinary citizen of Makkah reply to this message as they watched Othman destroy the idols?

❼ Muslims have no statues in any of their places of worship. Why not?

MAKING CONNECTIONS

❶ Makkah and Madinah are special places for Muslims. Is there a city which is very special to you? Write an article about your special city. Find out about places of interest and highlight these in your article. What makes this city so special?

❷ Have you ever done something difficult which you considered to be well worth the effort? How does it feel when you make a special effort to achieve something and it pays off?

❸ Nowadays pop stars, actors or football players might be considered as idols. Why? Who are your idols? In what ways do you idolise these people? Do you think this is the same or different as worshipping something? Would you consider any ordinary people to be your idols? Do you think having an idol is a good or a bad thing? Give reasons.

❹ After many years of conflict Muhammad had to resolve his difficulties with the people of Makkah and reach a compromise. Describe a time when you tried to resolve a conflict with someone by reaching a compromise. How helpful do you think Muhammad's approach would be in modern day conflicts between communities? Can you think of any times when world leaders have used such an approach?

stimulus
2 *Interpreting the Qur'an*

What the Qur'an says:

And proclaim the Pilgrimage among men: they will come to thee on foot and mounted on every kind of camel ... through deep and distant mountain highways. (Surah 22:27)

Then let them complete the rites prescribed for them, perform their vows, and again circumambulate the Ancient House. (Surah 22:29)

What this means for modern day Muslims:

Islam is now a worldwide faith. Some people still travel to Makkah on foot or by camel but millions have to use planes, trains, boats and cars or buses in order to get there. For many it is a long and expensive journey.

The Hajj lasts for several days. The first ritual or 'rite' which is performed is walking around the Ka'aba seven times anti-clockwise and this is repeated again at the end of the pilgrimage. During the days in between, Muslims perform rituals at a number of different places in and around Makkah.

What the Qur'an says:

And complete the Hajj in the service of Allah. But if you are prevented from completing it, send an offering for sacrifice ... and do not shave your heads until the offering reaches the place of sacrifice. (Surah 2:196)

For Hajj are the months well known. If any one undertakes that duty therein, Let there be no obscenity, nor wickedness, nor wrangling in the Hajj. (Surah 2:197)

It is no crime in you if you seek of the bounty of your Lord during pilgrimage. Then when you pour down from Mount Arafat, celebrate the praises of Allah at the Sacred Monument, and celebrate His praises as He has directed you, even though, before this, ye went astray. (Surah 2:198)

So when you have accomplished your holy rites, celebrate the praises of Allah, as you used to celebrate the praises of your fathers... (Surah 2:200)

What this means for modern day Muslims:

Near the end of the pilgrimage, animals are slaughtered and the food distributed amongst the people. It's a way of saying thanks to Allah but also a way of ensuring that everyone there is taken care of – even those who are poor and may have spent all they had just making the journey. Once the animals have been slaughtered, the men shave their heads.

There are very strict rules of conduct for Hajj. It is a sacred journey and the places visited are all holy sites. There should be not even a hint of violence, crime or even minor conflict amongst the pilgrims.

It was on Mount Arafat that Muhammad preached his very last sermon, so it is a very special place for the pilgrims to visit. At this place, Muslims pray and worship Allah from sunrise until sunset. Given that many pilgrims are quite weary by the time they reach here, a whole day on the mountain is a tremendous challenge for many. At sunset, everyone descends at once in order to head to Mina before returning to the Ka'aba to thank Allah for giving them the strength to complete the pilgrimage.

What the Qur'an says:

Behold! Safa and Marwa are among the Symbols of Allah. So if those who visit the House in the Season or at other times, should compass them round, it is no sin in them. (Surah 2:158)

What this means for modern day Muslims:

Safa and Marwa are two small hills just outside Makkah. The pilgrims re-enact Hagar's frantic search for water by repeatedly running between these two hills.

The Qur'an

FINDING OUT

❶ Find out how Muslims from Britain would get to Makkah today. How much would it cost? Would they need any injections before travelling to Makkah? What currency would they need for spending when they got there?

❷ What is the first ritual pilgrims perform on pilgrimage?

❸ Type the word 'Hajj' into a search engine like Google and find out more about the different rituals which Muslims perform. Some websites offer video clips or sound-bites.

❹ What sort of things might be considered as 'obscenity, wickedness or wrangling'? Why are these behaviours forbidden during Hajj? Design a poster of rules to remind pilgrims of the things which are not allowed.

❺ Explain why Muslims go to Mount Arafat. Why is it often a very challenging part of the pilgrimage?

❻ At Mina, pilgrims throw pebbles at three pillars which represent Satan. What do you think this ritual might symbolise?

❼ Ask your teacher to tell you the story of Hagar and her search for water in the desert. This story is well known to Muslims, Jews and Christians. Do you think Abraham was right to trust God and leave his wife and child alone in the middle of the desert?

❽ Has anyone in your class or school been on the pilgrimage to Makkah? Invite them to come along and tell you about their personal experience of the trip. You might be able to invite someone from a local mosque if there is no one in your school.

MAKING CONNECTIONS

❶ 'The Qur'an is like a manual for my life – it guides every aspect of my life' (a Muslim). What does this person mean when he says the Qur'an is like a manual? Is there a special book which has influenced and guided your thoughts or actions?

❷ Rituals are actions which are always performed in the same way. They usually feel important to the people performing them. Are there any rituals which you perform regularly? These might be related to religious beliefs or family celebrations or even just your everyday life.

❸ Have you ever been to a big football match or pop concert? What's it like being part of a huge crowd all with the same purpose in mind? Think about the noise or the singing/chanting. Describe the feeling of moving along as part of a crowd when you leave such an event.

❹ Are there any pilgrimage sites near where you live? Have you ever been to one or taken part in a pilgrimage? If so, prepare a talk for your class. Perhaps you might have photographs and/or special objects which you could bring along.

Thinking it over

❶ How useful is it to reenact events from history every year? What examples can you think of? Discuss the advantages and disadvantages of keeping the past alive.

❷ Hajj is a duty which all Muslims are expected to perform. What does it mean to have a 'sense of duty'? Do you feel any sense of duty in your life? Is a sense of duty a good thing? In what ways might having a sense of duty restrict our individual freedom? What duties have all humans to the planet, to other creatures and to other people?

❸ Abraham left Hagar and Ishmael in the desert because he had faith in God. What does it means to have *faith* in someone or something? Can you think of modern examples of people who have shown a similar faith in God? Is it easy or difficult to have such faith? Do you have faith in anyone or anything special? How does this faith help you in your life?

❹ During Hajj there are lots of opportunities for Muslims to think about things they have done wrong in life and to ask forgiveness for their sins. The end of Hajj is like a new beginning. Should everyone have the opportunity to make a fresh start at least once in their life? Are there any actions which should not be forgiven, even by God?

stimulus
3 *Postcards from Makkah*

Hi Folks

What an amazing sight! I've never seen so many people! There must have been at least two million people there. It was exciting and a bit scary – everyone moving around the Ka'aba trying to touch the Black Stone. Did you know that it was meant to have been given to Ishmael by the angel Jibrel? At one point a poor woman tripped and fell over. I thought she would be trampled to death like some people have been! I held my breath and prayed to Allah until I saw her being helped to her feet again. I am totally in awe of everything here!

See you soon love Rasmia.

Hi Mum

Don't worry I'm managing fine even with the wheelchair. I didn't realise there was an actual corridor built between the two hills, did you? It meant we didn't get too much of the scorching hot sun. There's even a special 'slow lane' for folk like me in wheelchairs or on crutches or just old and not able to move fast! Everyone has been so kind. Yesterday a lovely young student from Kenya pushed me along for a wee while so that Dad could have a rest. I'm so glad you persuaded me to come, I'm loving it.

Wish you were here though, your loving son, Yusuf.

Dear Sasha

This was the scariest moment of the whole trip for me, yet I wouldn't have missed it for the world! The night before we had slept out under the stars at Muzdalifah and in the morning collected handfuls of small pebbles to throw at the pillars. Remember I told you it's a way of showing that we don't want Satan to be a part of our lives? When we got to Mina it was all a bit mad! The sound of thousands of pilgrims all calling out 'Allahu Akbar'(God is the Greatest) will stay with me forever. It was so hot and people were crushed so tightly together I would have fallen over if Ali hadn't been holding me so tight. We were lucky to get near to the pillars so that I was able to hit them with some of my pebbles, but the down side of that was being hit in the head and back by the pebbles of those behind us! No lasting damage done though! Can't wait to tell you the rest when I get home.

Big Hug, Samia

Dear Malik

It has been the experience of a lifetime just as you said it would be. Makkah is certainly a city of contrast. As you can see, on the one hand it is a thriving, modern, vibrant commercial centre and yet it is also a city of peace and immense spirituality. As soon as we had our passports checked and were allowed to enter the sacred district around the Great Mosque, I felt the change. We were all there for the same simple purpose – to praise Allah. I feel a real strength in my faith having been here and an inner peace which I pray will be with me until the day I die. I know that you have sacrificed much for me to be here, I thank you for everything, but especially for introducing me to Islam.

Your faithful and loving wife, Irene.

❶ Copy and complete this table using information from the postcards written during Hajj. Although some sections have been started for you, you can add anything else you think is important.

Name	A lasting memory of Hajj	Feelings about Hajj
Rasmia		Amazed and overwhelmed
Yusuf	The 'slow lane'	
Samia		Scared but excited too
Irene	Makkah is a city of contrasts	

❷ Here are some statements of advice about Hajj. Who do you think made each statement; Rasmia, Yusuf, Samia or Irene? Write out the statement with the name of the correct person beside it. Which piece of advice do you think is most important? Give a reason for your choice.

a) 'There's no need to worry, everyone can take part. It doesn't matter what your limitations are.'

b) 'Even if you were not born a Muslim you will be accepted if you try your best to participate fully in all the rituals.'

c) 'It's your husband's duty to protect you – make sure he does just that!'

d) 'It's right in the corner of the Ka'aba, get as close to it as you can, kissing it will bring you a lot of good fortune.'

e) 'Remember to take valid identification, you won't get near the Ka'aba unless you can prove you are a Muslim.'

f) 'Never mind the tent, just sleep under the stars, it's magical'

❸ Find out why non-Muslims are not allowed near the Ka'aba. Are the Muslim authorities right to keep tourists away? Give a reason for your answer.

❹ Which of the following objects do you think pilgrims would pack for Hajj? Explain why they might or might not need each one.

- Qur'an
- camera
- toothbrush
- sleeping bag
- money
- hat
- suncream
- binoculars
- map & compass
- musical instrument

❺ What does the phrase 'Allahu Akbar' mean? Try to find out about other times that Muslims might use this phrase.

❻ Imagine that you are a reporter and have been asked to write a piece entitled 'The Challenge of Hajj'. Use information from the postcards to get you started. Write an article which highlights why Hajj is a real achievement for many Muslims. Think carefully about what might make it a very difficult few days indeed. Explain why those who complete the full pilgrimage are given the special title Hajji for the rest of their life.

❼ Conduct a one-minute brainstorming session entitled 'The Joy of Hajj'. Write down as many positive things about Hajj as you can think of. Which three things on your list seem most important? Explain why.

MAKING CONNECTIONS

❶ When was the last time you went on a long journey? What did you take with you? What was the purpose of the journey? Were there any surprises either during the journey or when you got to your destination? Was the journey a positive experience?

❷ Irene said that being on pilgrimage gave her 'an inner peace'. Have you ever had a similar experience? How did it feel? When did it happen? Would you like to have such an experience?

Thinking it over

❶ Irene converted to Islam. What does that mean? Some people say, 'If you are born into one religion, that should be your religion until you die'. Do you agree or disagree? Why might someone want to convert to a new religion? How easy would it be to give up a religion which you have been brought up to follow? Would your faith be stronger if you had chosen it for yourself rather than following your parents' beliefs?

❷ Muslims like to conduct Hajj in a kind of private way without tourists and non-Muslims watching everything they are doing. Does the information available on the Internet and in books and on video go against this principle?

❸ Samia writes 'we don't want Satan to be part of our lives'. What do you think Samia means? Do you think Satan exists? Where does evil come from? What is the ritual at Mina which shows Muslims try to resist evil? Do you think it is a helpful ritual?

❹ If something is potentially quite dangerous, does that make it more appealing? Why do people often take huge risks in order to achieve their lifetime goals? Can you give some examples of people who have done so?

stimulus 4 Ihram

All Muslims performing Hajj must respect Ihram. Ihram refers to the sacred physical and mental state of the pilgrim. It involves taking off normal clothes and wearing special garments so that everyone looks the same; and following the Ihram rules.

Clothing

Male pilgrims are expected to wear only two pieces of unsewn cloth wrapped and folded around the body with one shoulder left bare. No metal should be worn, not even a safety pin to hold the fabric together. They usually wear a simple pair of sandals and perhaps a simple belt tied around their waist. Women may wear anything they like as long as they are modestly dressed. They usually wear a simple white dress and headscarf unless they have a particular national dress which fits the bill.

Although the Qur'an does not give any ruling about what to wear for Hajj, Muslims believe that it is important that every pilgrim is given equal status during Hajj. When men and women change into the garments of Ihram it is impossible to tell who is rich and who is poor.

Muslim men wearing the white garments of Ihram

Ihram Rules

- *There should be no hair or nails trimming because on Hajj nature should not be interfered with.*
- *No perfume is allowed, including scented soap.*
- *Sexual intercourse is not permitted.*
- *Only women are allowed to wear something which touches their head but they are forbidden to cover their face unless they are in the company of male strangers.*
- *Men should leave their heads uncovered as a sign of humility but if they need protection from the sun they should carry an umbrella.*
- *You are not allowed to kill anything. This even includes flies, mosquitoes or head-lice!*
- *There should be no dishonest or arrogant behaviour.*
- *As a sign of love of nature no plants should be uprooted.*
- *There should be no loss of temper or quarrelling.*

Dear Sir

Please allow me to use the pages of your newspaper to raise some objections about the wearing of Ihram during Hajj. As a devout Muslim who reads the Holy Qur'an daily, I am confused by the insistence on this code of dress for pilgrims. Nowhere in the Qur'an does Allah proclaim such a uniform. On the contrary, Surah 7:32 quite clearly states: 'O children of Adam take 'Zeenatakom' (your adornments) to EVERY Masjid, and eat and drink moderately.' So how can it be right to make an exception for the Great Mosque in Makkah? It seems more appropriate to me that we should wear our best clothes and show how proud we are of our faith. We should celebrate this occasion with as much joy and carnival as possible. The poor stand side by side with their rich neighbours in every mosque during Friday prayers. If they can feel at one with their fellow worshippers then regardless of how they are dressed, then surely the same could be said of Hajj.
Yours sincerely

Confused Believer

Dear Sir

I read last week's letter from 'Confused Believer' with interest and wondered how the writer might call himself by such a contradiction. How can anyone who questions the wearing of Ihram consider themselves to be a 'Believer' of Islam? While I wish him no harm, it is with true dedication to my faith that I wish to correct some of the objections he raised. It is true that the Qur'an does not specify the wearing of Ihram, but it clearly does tell us to dress modestly. The guidelines for Ihram are contained in Hadith, but this does not mean they should be optional. The teachings of the Prophet are most valuable and we need to understand that any guidance given in Hadith is based on sound wisdom and experience. Hajj is not merely a festive occasion as your writer seemed to suggest. It is a spiritual journey and as such is to be taken on board in a most serious manner. It is right to prepare oneself thoroughly and this includes changing into a garment which signifies purity of intention as well as equality between all pilgrims. It is truly appropriate dress for the occasion.
Yours sincerely

Mr Ali, Imam, Anytown Mosque.

❶ Present some information about Ihram as a set of road signs which could be posted along the route to Makkah:
- Oblong signs with a black border are information.
- Red Triangles are warning symbols.
- Red circles are things you should do.
- Red circles with a line through them are things you should avoid.

❷ Explain the reasons for the rules about clothing on pilgrimage.

❸ Why does 'Confused Believer' object to the wearing of Ihram?

❹ Why does Mr Ali think that the title 'Confused Believer' is a contradiction'?

❺ Imagine a meeting between 'Confused Believer' and Mr Ali, the Imam of Anytown Mosque. Write a script of their conversation. You could act out the meeting and use the sketch as the starting point for a class debate about this issue. Take a vote and see which letter has most support from your class.

stimulus 5 Top tips for pilgrims

There are literally thousands of travel agents and tour companies offering their services to Muslims intending to take part in Hajj. Here are some of the best bits of practical advice for modern day pilgrims.

1 Buy all the essential Hajj items in your own country before departure. In Muslim countries you can usually get everything as a set. If you wait until you get to Makkah you will probably find it quite expensive.

2 Everyone must have a guide, even independent travellers. This is to make sure you perform the rituals properly and that you don't get lost or in any kind of difficulty during Hajj. It is often best to travel as part of a group.

3 Bring a small cloth bag which you can easily identify. This is to keep your shoes in when you need to remove them. But don't be surprised if you still lose them amongst the thousands of pairs outside the Great Mosque!

4 Bring a small mat so that you can sit or lie down whenever you need a rest. This can be useful for your night at Muzdalifah since the desert floor is quite uncomfortable!

5 Be prepared to share your accommodation with strangers unless your whole family books a room together. Makkah is a very busy place during Hajj.

6 Remember to get a receipt when you pay the cost of your animal sacrifice. Ask for a slaughter on the first day and make a note of the time so you don't miss it!

7 If you want to fill containers with Zam Zam water to bring home, allow plenty of time for doing this. There can be long queues at the taps. You would be well advised to go at three or four in the morning.

8 Beware of pickpockets! Yes, even in the Mosque itself and especially when circling the Ka'aba. Unfortunately, not all Muslims in Makkah are there for Hajj!

9 Do give money to the poor but watch out for fake beggars and con-artists. Some people will try to get your money by telling you sad stories of how they have been robbed and are stranded.

10 In Arafat, drinks and bags of food are provided free of charge. Elsewhere you will need to buy food but prices are usually quite reasonable except in Mina.

11 Take only essential medicines with you, free check ups and health care are available if required.

12 When you are circling the Ka'aba do not try to touch it. Be aware that the authorities often put perfume on it to discourage people from trying to get so close all at once. You can still touch or kiss the Black Stone.

FINDING OUT

❶ What qualities do you think a Hajj guide would need? Write down three personal qualities and explain why you think these are essential for this job.

❷ Why do Muslims remove their shoes for worship? Why are pilgrims likely to lose their shoes in Makkah?

❸ Find out more about the ritual slaughtering of animals during Hajj. Write a brief report on the rules which govern this practice.

❹ What evidence is there that not everyone in Makkah during Hajj is being faithful to Allah? Why might Makkah be described as a haven for these people? Should they be given harsher punishments than normal because they are taking advantage of pilgrims?

❺ Suggest three ways that the Muslim authorities try to take good care of the pilgrims.

❻ Why might someone who had never been on Hajj find these tips valuable? What impression of Hajj do they help to give?

Thinking it over

❶ What do you want the experience of your lifetime to be? Is it important to have a goal in life? How might having a goal help to keep you motivated during your life?

❷ Explain how making the Hajj involves a lot of time, effort and upheaval. Why would a Muslim say it was all worthwhile? What would you be willing to do and sacrifice in order to achieve your goal in life?

❸ 'The Hajj is now too touristy, and this lessens its meaning. It makes going too easy.'

'The tourist industry does a good job, it helps many Muslims go on Hajj who previously would not have managed to go.'

Which of these statements do you agree with more? Explain your answer?

Ummah

The Ummah is often called 'the brotherhood of Islam'. It's a word which sums up the idea that Muslims from all over the world feel they are part of the same family. There is a sense of unity amongst Muslims no matter which part of the world they live in. Muslims in Britain feel that they have a special bond with Muslims in other countries because of their shared belief in Allah and the practice of Islam.

IN THIS SECTION YOU WILL BE ASKED TO THINK ABOUT...

✓ Unity
✓ Community
✓ Obligation
✓ Family

stimulus 1

Letter from Zaina to her aunt in America

Dear Auntie Ameena

as – Salamu – 'alaykum

How have you settled into life in Washington? It must be an exciting city to live in, with the White House and all the museums and everything. I hope you will be very happy in your new life. Although we miss you loads and I'm sure you miss us, I know you will soon find friends. I recently read that Islam is the fastest growing religion in the USA so there is bound to be a mosque that you can go to where you will meet other Muslim families. Don't worry though, we will always think of you as part of our family even if you are far away. We are connected by blood but also connected by faith.

There have been quite a few things happening at this end lately. We have had a lot of visitors coming and going and I have been meeting Muslim young people from different parts of the world. As you know, there are a lot of students from Glasgow University who attend the mosque. Recently they held a special 'getting to know us event'. Each group puts up a wee stall telling us a bit about their country with photos of mosques and, much to my delight, some samples of food which we were able to taste. So many countries were represented I can't remember them all, but I do remember talking to a young medical student from your homeland, Tunisia.

What I found really interesting was that although there were students from Pakistan, Turkey, Saudi Arabia and some other Muslim countries, there were also two students from Norway, a boy from Ireland, a wee group from India, two girls from Australia and a really good-looking boy called Rana from Bangladesh!

The atmosphere was wonderful, everyone was very friendly and just happy to share in being part of the same community. It not only gave us a chance to welcome them to Glasgow but also gave them a chance to get to know each other. I'm sure everyone went home that night with at least one new phone number or email address! Grandad told me that the word for this is Ummah. He says it's one of the best things about being a Muslim. No matter where you go in the world you will always find a welcome within the brotherhood of Islam and this will make your faith in Allah even stronger. I hope that is true for you in the USA.

Please write to me soon and tell me all about your new life.

Lots of love and hugs

Your loving niece Zaina xxx

FINDING OUT

❶ Why is Zaina not worried that her Aunt Ameena will be lonely in Washington?

❷ What do you think she means by the phrase 'we are connected by blood but also by faith'?

❸ Why are there so many Muslim students attending the mosque in Glasgow?

❹ What sort of event does Zaina say she has been to lately? Give two reasons why she enjoyed herself.

❺ Ask your teacher to give you a blank map of the world to stick in your jotter. Use an atlas to find the countries where all the students Zaina met came from. Mark them on your map. Remember to also mark on the USA where Zaina's auntie lives.

❻ State two things which made this event useful for the Muslim students.

❼ What does the word Ummah mean? Why did Zaina's grandad use it to describe her recent experience?

❽ How might being a member of the Ummah help Muslims who travel to live in other countries around the world?

❾ Zaina starts her letter with the traditional Muslim greeting. It means 'peace be with you'. Write out the greeting in Arabic and in English. Why do you think she starts her letter in this way?

MAKING CONNECTIONS

❶ Do you have any friends or family who have gone to live abroad or to another part of the United Kingdom? Do you think it is important to keep in touch with family and friends who live far away? Give reasons for your answer.

❷ The mosque is a meeting place for Muslims as well as a place of worship. Make a list of meeting places in your community. Who uses these places? What sorts of activities take place there? How are they similar or different from a mosque?

❸ Think about the people in these pictures. Where would you advise them to go in order to meet like-minded people and make new friends?

I have been very lonely since my husband died. My family all live far away.

Having the baby is wonderful, but I miss the company of my workmates.

My parents moved here because of work. Great for them, but I miss my friends. I have no social life here.

The course I am studying is great, but I wish I could meet some people who are not medical students!

❹ As pupils you are all members of the same school community. How do you show you belong to the same community? What are the advantages of feeling that you belong to a community?

 stimulus 2 *Earthquake in Asia*

On 8th October 2005, a major earthquake struck Pakistan and northern India. The earthquake measured 7.6 on the Richter Scale and devastated communities in Kashmir, Pakistan, India and even as far as Afghanistan. More than 75,000 people were killed and thousands more were injured. Approximately two million people were made homeless and in some areas whole villages were completely demolished. The majority of those affected by the earthquake were Muslims. As news of the disaster quickly spread, special prayer sessions were arranged in mosques throughout the world and appeals were made for much needed funding and supplies. The worldwide community of Islam responded with speed and compassion to support their fellow Muslims in this time of need.

British Muslims Send Condolences and Aid to Earthquake Victims in Kashmir, Pakistan and India

Pakistani ex-pats in Australia pray for quake victims

American Muslims raise funds for quake victims

Muslims in Holland pray for earthquake victims

Muslims in Baramullah and Ahmedabad held prayers on Saturday for the victims of the massive earthquake that struck South Asia

Pakistani worshippers attend the first Friday prayers after South Asia's earthquake

Muslims in London launch earthquake appeal

FINDING OUT

❶ What happened in October 2005 to destroy many Muslim communities in Asia?

❷ Use the Internet to find out more about this disaster and write your own newspaper report describing what happened.

❸ How did the Muslim community in other parts of the world respond to this crisis? In what ways does this illustrate the concept of Ummah?

❹ Suggest two reasons why Muslims in London would wish to raise funds for the earthquake victims.

❺ What does it mean to show 'compassion'? Why is compassion important at a time of such crisis?

❻ Imagine that you are the Imam (religious leader) at your local mosque. You need to make an appeal asking your congregation to help those hurt in the earthquake. Write the speech you will give at Friday prayers when most people will attend the mosque. Remember to emphasise the belief that you are all part of the same family and that looking after each other is something Allah demands of all Muslims.

❼ Think about the people who survived the earthquake. What things would they need urgently? What sort of immediate aid could Muslim communities send them? Design a poster appealing for the different types of aid required.

MAKING CONNECTIONS

❶ Look at the following pictures of people.

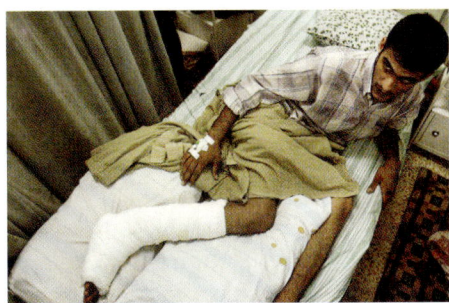

What do you think has happened to them? How do you feel when you think about these people? Imagine you are one of these people. Write a story describing what has happened to you and the kind of help you need from others.

❷ Teams of people worked together to help the earthquake victims in 2005. Have you ever been part of a team working on a project?

Copy and complete this table in your jotter;

Times when it is useful to have a team	Advantages of working as a team

❸ Copy this drawing in the centre of your page. Around the drawing use one colour of pen to write words to show the things people from different parts of the world have in common with each other and another thing to write the things which you think are different about people from different parts of the world.

❹ Who are the people in need in your community? What is being done to help them? Investigate the work of a charity that does work in your local community and invite someone from that charity in to speak to your class.

❺ Think of ways that your class could help the charity you have investigated. You might do some fundraising or act as volunteers at a local event or collect things to give to people in need like food, clothes, toys, household goods etc. Try to get as many people involved as you can so that you have a team of people working together. Write a report about your achievements as a team for the school magazine or a local newspaper.

stimulus 3 *Zakat*

Zakat is the third Pillar of Islam. All adult Muslims who are mentally stable, free and financially able must pay Zakat every year. Zakat is a sum of money which is then used to help those in need. When the Zakat is due, Muslims are obliged to calculate the money they have and give 2.5 per cent of any money which is not needed to support the family. Muslims are also encouraged to give extra Zakat whenever they can afford to do so.

Sayings of the Prophet Muhammad about Zakat

'The best charity is to feed an empty stomach.'

'Whosoever clothes another Muslim, Allah will clothe him on the Day of Judgement with clothes of Heaven.'

'Indeed, an ignorant man who is generous is dearer to God than a worshipper who is miserly.'

'Every good, done for the rich or the poor, is charity.'

'...wealth is sweet fruit, and whoever takes it without greed, God will bless it for him, but whoever takes it with greed...will be like someone who eats but is never satisfied.'

'The nation that does not pay Zakat, Allah afflicts famine on them.'

Sheikh Musif told a story about Zakat

A beggar was sitting in the streets outside the Ka'aba in Makkah.
A rich man walked past him on his way to his Mercedes. As the man got into car the beggar called out 'Please help me, for the sake of Allah'.

The man replied 'Allah will provide' to which the beggar responded 'I know that you fool!' The man got into his car and drove away.

A poor African woman sitting in street selling cloth saw what had happened. She didn't have a lot of money, but she pulled out one Riyal and placed it in the hands of the beggar. He smiled and went on his way.

Meanwhile, the man in the Mercedes felt guilty as he drove home. He decided to turn the car around and go back to the beggar. As he approached the spot where he had met the beggar before, he pulled ten riyals out of his wallet. However, the beggar had gone and the man could not find him.

What could he do? He had pulled out the money intending to give for the sake of Allah and could not in good conscience put it straight back in his wallet. He found the nearest person he could and put the ten riyal note in her lap.

As the rich man walked away, the ten riyals sat in the lap of the African woman who had given to the beggar.

The benefits of Zakat

- Obeying God.
- Helping a person acknowledge that everything comes from God on loan and that humans do not really own anything ourselves.
- Understanding that since humans cannot take anything with them when they die they need not cling to it.
- Acknowledging that whether humans are rich or poor is God's choice. So people should help those He has chosen to make poor.
- Learning self-discipline.
- Freeing oneself from the love of possessions and greed.
- Freeing oneself from the love of money.
- Freeing oneself from love of oneself.
- Behaving honestly.

❶ How much is every Muslim obliged to give for Zakat?

❷ What is Zakat used for?

❸ What does it mean to be 'obliged' to do something?

❹ Look at the sayings of Prophet Muhammad and try to explain why Muslims are obliged to give Zakat.

❺ What did Prophet Muhammad say was 'the best charity'?

❻ Look at Sheikh Musif's story about Zakat.
   a) Why did the rich man not give to the beggar at first?
   b) What made the African woman's gift so special?
   c) What do you think made the rich man feel guilty?
   d) How do you think the African woman will feel about receiving the ten riyals?
   e) What do you think is the lesson from this story?

❼ Make up your own version of the story which Shiekh Musif told. Give your story a local setting and make the characters people that you would see in your own town. Use pictures to create your own storyboard.

❽ Which of the benefits of Zakat do you think would seem the most important to a Muslim? Which do you think would seem most important to a non-Muslim? Make a list of your top five benefits of Zakat.

MAKING CONNECTIONS

❶ Muslims are obliged to give Zakat. It's like a duty they must keep. What sort of obligations might the following people have?
   • Parents.
   • Teachers.
   • Politicians.
   • Pupils.
   • Brothers and sisters.
   • The police.

❷ Make a spider diagram showing the particular duties which you have towards others in your life.

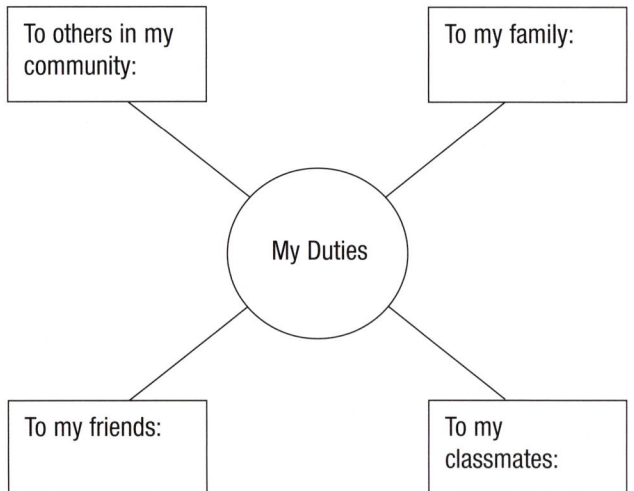

Thinking it over

❶ 'My most important duty is to look after myself.' How would a Muslim respond to this statement? What are the advantages of thinking of others before ourselves? In what ways might our society be improved if people thought more about others and less about themselves?

❷ Do we live in a selfish society? Do you think people do enough to help other people? Do people really care about those who are less fortunate?

❸ Zakat doesn't have to be money. If people are poor themselves, how can they still give Zakat? How will giving Zakat help Muslims to feel part of the Ummah?

❹ 'People today think too much about their own rights and not enough about their duties and responsibilities.' Why do some people argue this? Do you agree?

Friday prayers at the mosque

stimulus **4**

Mark: Ali why are you always late for school on Friday afternoons?

Ali: On Fridays at noon I go to pray at the Mosque. We have special prayers then every week.

Mark: Why a Friday?

Ali: It was declared as the holy day by Prophet Muhammad PBUH and the Qur'an tells us we must gather together for prayers on that day.

Mark: But I thought you prayed five times every day?

Ali: Yes we do, but Friday is different. Although we might choose to go to the mosque for other prayer times, we don't have to; you can pray at home, school or work if that's more appropriate for you. On Fridays though there is a special sermon preached by the Imam and everyone who can is obliged to attend. When everyone is there it helps you to remember that you are part of a whole community. Usually there are hundreds of people there and the mosque is packed full of worshippers.

Mark: So how do you fit everyone in? The mosque here isn't that big is it?

Ali: It's easy to fit a lot of people into a mosque because when we pray we are in rows all very close together. Because of the prayer movements there are no chairs to take up space between us. We begin by standing shoulder to shoulder. It reminds

O ye who believe! When the call is proclaimed to prayer on Friday [the Day of Assembly], hasten earnestly to the Remembrance of Allah, and leave off business and traffic: that is best for you if ye but knew! (Surah 62:9)

us that we are united and that together our faith is stronger. It's a symbol of the continual support we give to one another as members of the Ummah.

Mark: I've heard about that, it's like a big family isn't it?

Ali: Yes, when you enter the prayer hall you must take your place next to the person who has entered just before you. It doesn't matter if you know him personally or not or if he is wearing rags or riches. We are taught to accept each other as members of the same family. Sometimes you will find kings or presidents standing next to the poorest men in the community, but they are united in their faith in Allah and therefore pray together.

Mark: What if you are a newcomer or a visitor to the area?

Ali: It doesn't matter where you come from, you simply take your place in line. You are a Muslim and that is all that matters. I could go into any mosque in the world to say prayers and know I would be made welcome. It's also amazing for me to think that while I am praying here, there are Muslims all over the UK praying at exactly the same time and in exactly the same way.

Mark: Wow I hadn't thought of that! Doesn't that make you feel part of something really big?

Ali: The sense of belonging is amazing and especially on Fridays during these special prayers. Standing next to my Dad and my brothers and seeing my uncles, neighbours, friends and other members of the community makes me feel very safe and secure. I am a part of something very special indeed.

Mark: I wish I could feel like that. I just have to come straight back to school after lunch on Fridays! Maybe I'll come to the Mosque with you sometime.

FINDING OUT

❶ Why do most Muslims try to attend the mosque at noon on Fridays?

❷ Look at the passage from the Qur'an in Stimulus 4. Why might it be good for Muslims to live or work near a mosque?

❸ State two things which make the Friday prayer different from all other prayer times.

❹ How does praying together make Muslims feel part of the Ummah?

❺ Ali says you might find kings and poor people standing next to each other in prayer. Why would Muslims say that was a good thing?

❻ Write down the words Ali uses to describe his feelings during the Friday prayer. Explain what it is that makes him feel this way.

❼ How does Ali know he will be made welcome in any mosque in any part of the world?

❽ Ask your teacher to show you a video of Muslims praying in the mosque. Try to imagine what it would be like to be there.

MAKING CONNECTIONS

1 Muslims belong to the Ummah. The symbol of the Ummah is the star and crescent moon. Think of a group that you belong to. Design a badge with a special symbol that all members of your group could wear. Your badge should be a way to express the unity of your group.

2 Friday noon is a special time for Muslims. Do you have any special times in the week? Are there any regular events which you always try to be at? How do these things help to make your week special? How do you feel if you have to miss out one week?

3 When was the last time you went to a big family gathering? What do you like/dislike about going to family events? Why are family gatherings important?

4 Are there places outside of your hometown where you know you would be welcomed – perhaps where other family members live, or because you are a member of a club which has connections with other countries? How do you think they would make you feel welcome? In what ways is it good to know that you will be welcome in other places besides your own home?

Thinking it over

1 Being part of the Ummah means that Muslims give a great deal of support to each other. Think of the different ways Muslims support each other. Try to list different types of support under each of the words below. Which of the following words do you think best describes the support Muslims get from other members of the Ummah?

Emotional   Financial
Spiritual   Practical

2 'Believers are like parts of a building; each part supports the others.'

'If any single part of the body aches, the whole body feels the effects of it and rushes to its relief.'

Explain how each quote teaches about the Muslim idea of Ummah. Which quote do you think explains Ummah best? Why?

3 Here are some words to describe feelings:

secure   loved   lonely   jealous
anxious   relieved scared   safe

Which of these feelings would most likely apply to Muslims who believe they belong to the Ummah? How do you think the concept of Ummah helps Muslims to feel stronger in their faith?

4 What is more important:

a) being free to express your own individuality?
b) conforming to the beliefs and practices of the community you want to be part of?

Does there have to be a conflict between the two? Are there ways in which we can express our individuality but still be part of a community?

5 Ummah is an ideal – something to aim for. What do you think this means? Why might Muslims find it difficult to achieve perfect Ummah?

Sikhism

The Khalsa

The Khalsa is the community of those Sikhs who have undergone the initiation ceremony. This section explores the beginning of the Khalsa and considers what it means for a Sikh to belong to the Khalsa.

IN THIS SECTION YOU WILL BE ASKED TO THINK ABOUT...

✓ Commitment
✓ Loyalty
✓ Belonging
✓ Acceptance
✓ Identity

stimulus 1 — The beginning of the Khalsa

The Sikh Khalsa was formed in April 1699. At the time, the leader of the Sikhs was Guru Gobind Singh. The Guru's father had been beheaded for speaking up for people of a different religion. These were Hindus who were being persecuted. This had scared all the Sikhs. They thought they might be the next to be killed. Gobind Singh taught Sikhs that they should stand up for their beliefs. They should never be frightened of showing they were Sikhs. He decided to put them to the test. On a festival day he called together all the Sikh community. He stood in front of them, sword in hand and asked if any Sikh was prepared to die for their beliefs. There

was silence. Eventually one man bravely stepped forward.

The Guru took him into the tent. Then he came out alone, his sword covered in blood. He asked for a second volunteer. Again one man came forward. This happened five times. On each occasion the Guru came out of the tent with his blood-soaked sword. Then the Guru went into the tent. To the crowd's joy he came out with all five men. They had turbans on their heads. The Guru called these five Sikhs the Panj Pyare. This means 'the beloved five'. Later that day the Guru sprinkled a sugar-water solution on their heads as a sign of initiation. He told them that they were the first members of a new community of equals, the Khalsa, and that their task was to serve people and fight for justice for all people, whatever their religion.

1. When was the Sikh Khalsa formed and who was leader of the Sikhs at the time?

2. Why were Sikhs frightened at this time?

3. Look at the drawing. What part of the story does it tell?

4. Why do you think the Guru called the five volunteers the 'beloved five'?

5. Explain what the Khalsa is and describe how the first members were initiated into the Khalsa.

6. Imagine you were present on the day the Khalsa was formed. Write three paragraphs. In the first describe what happened in your own words. In the second explain how you felt. In the third explain why it was an important day for Sikhs.

7. Look at the picture of Guru Gobind Singh and think about the part Guru Gobind Singh played in the story. Choose two of the words below which you think describes what sort of person he was. Explain your choices.

brave   eccentric   demanding
belligerent   committed   calm   holy

MAKING CONNECTIONS

1. The beloved five were prepared to die for their beliefs. What other people have been prepared to die for their beliefs? (Clue: war; martyrs.)

2. What might you be prepared to die for? Complete the chart below

Would you be prepared to die for	Yes/No/It depends	Reason
Your family?		
A friend?		
Your country?		
Your beliefs/religion?		

2 Joining the Khalsa today

When Sikhs join the Khalsa today they go through a special initiation ceremony called the **Amrit ceremony**. During the ceremony they are sprinkled with a solution of sugar and water called Amrit. It is a sign that they have become adult members of the Sikh community, the Khalsa. At this ceremony Sikhs commit themselves to the teachings of Sikhism and agree to wear the five Ks.

Kesh
Uncut hair. This is a sign of accepting God's will. Sikhs wear a turban to keep the hair in place.

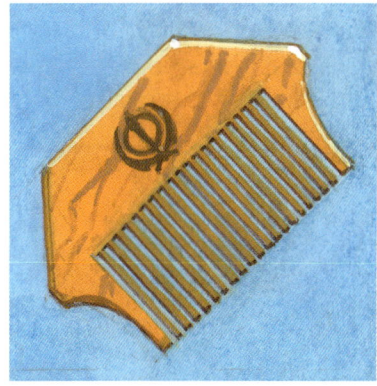

Kangha
A small wooden comb. This is used to keep the hair neat and tidy. It is a sign of discipline because keeping long hair tidy takes time and effort.

Kara
Steel Bangle. Its circular shape reminds Sikhs of the oneness of God. Just as a circle has no

beginning and no end, God has no beginning and no end.

Kachs
Shorts. These are easier to run in than the dhoti, the traditional Indian garment. It is a sign of freedom and good moral character.

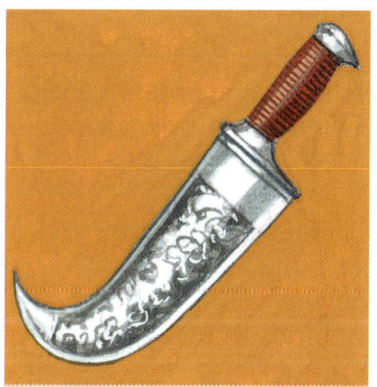

Kirpan
A small sword. This is a sign of the need for courage and the need to protect the weak.

A male Sikh will use the name Singh (meaning Lion) as a reminder of the need for courage. A female Sikh will use the name Kaur (meaning Princess) to emphasise the importance of dignity. Using the same name is a sign of equality.

❶ The chart below is about the five Ks. Copy it into your jotter and complete it

	Uncut hair	A sign that Sikhs accept God's will
Kangha		A sign of discipline
	Steel bracelet	
Kachs		
		A symbol of courage and self defence

❷ To show they are committed to the Sikh way of life Sikhs promise to uphold certain principles, for example:
- Do not steal.
- Do not practise astrology.
- Do not commit adultery.
- Do not use tobacco or alcohol.

The following statements represent the beliefs that lie behind these principles. Match each principle with one of the statements:
- Be faithful to the person you married.
- Look after your body.
- Earn money honestly.
- Trust in God and not the stars.

Which of these principles do you think Sikhs living today in the United Kingdom might find hard to keep? Why?

❸ In pairs brainstorm the words 'lion' and princess'. Write down all the words and ideas you can think of. What does calling men 'lion' and women 'princess' teach us about Sikh beliefs about the qualities men and women should show in their lives?

MAKING CONNECTIONS

❶ What people wear often tells us something about them. Explain, with examples, how each of the following might influence what a person wears:
- The school a person attends.
- A person's job.
- The organisation a person belongs to.
- The country a person belongs to.
- The religious group a person belongs to.

❷ Do you think what you wear expresses something about the kind of person you are? Can you give examples?

❸ Have you ever gone through an initiation ceremony, for example, to join a gang, to become a member of an organisation such as the guides or scouts, within a religious tradition? How did you feel afterwards? Did you think it was worthwhile?

Thinking it over

❶ What does it mean to be committed? Do you think it is easy or difficult to commit yourself to something?

❷ Do you think people sometimes commit themselves to doing something just because they find it easy? Why do you think that is? Should people also commit themselves to things that are difficult? What makes you say that?

❸ What kind of things weaken people's commitment to stick to what they intended? What can people do about this?

❹ What do you think you could commit your life to? How might you succeed in this?

❺ Wearing the five Ks indicates that the following values are important in a Sikh's life.

Discipline   Loyalty   Freedom
Courage   Protecting the weak

Do you think these are important for all people as well as Sikhs. Why/why not? Which one do you think is most important for you? Why?

stimulus 3 *The Amrit Ceremony*

A class of S1 pupils were given the chance to find out more about the Amrit Ceremony.

> Who can be initiated?

> The Amrit ceremony is open to men and women of any country and race. Those being initiated have to be old enough to understand the importance of what they are doing because during the ceremony they have to promise they will follow the Sikh way of life.

> Where does the Amrit ceremony take place?

> The Amrit ceremony takes place in the Gurdwara (Sikh place of worship) and in the presence of the Sikh Holy Book, the Guru Granth Sahib. In fact the opening of the Guru Granth Sahib marks the beginning of the ceremony.

> Who carries out the ceremony?

> It is carried out by five Sikhs. They are known as the Panj Pyare and they will be wearing the 5Ks. Before the ceremony begins those being initiated will have bathed, washed their hair, put on clean clothes and will also be wearing the 5Ks.

Why is the ceremony called the Amrit Ceremony?

Do those being initiated have to make any promises or vows?

Amrit is a solution of sugar and water and it plays an important part in the ceremony. Sugar is seen as a symbol of sweetness and human compassion.

Those who have been initiated have to repeat the Mool Mantra, the first verse in the Guru Granth Sahib, five times and they agree to follow the Sikh way of life. The ceremony ends with prayers and those initiated are declared members of the Khalsa.

How is Amrit prepared?

What do Sikhs pray for in their final prayers?

The Panj Pyare prepare the amrit. They fill a large iron bowl with water and sweeten it with lumps of sugar. The Panj Pyare kneel around the bowl with their right knee on the ground and the left raised. While they recite Sikh prayers and hymns, one of them stirs the water continuously with a Khanda, a double edged sword.

Part of the prayer is to remind them of Sikhs in the past who have been faithful and loyal to the Sikh faith, even in times of persecution.

What happens when the amrit is ready?

The amrit is then given to those being initiated. Each person being initiated comes forward one by one and kneels down. Each in turn says:

Waheguru Ji Ka Khalsa (The Khalsa is devoted to God)
Waheguru Ji Ki Fateh (So the victory is to the Almighty God)

They are each given a handful of amrit to drink and then the amrit is sprinkled five times on their eyes and hair.

Extract from the final prayers

Think of the glorious deeds of the five beloved ones…
Think of those who cleansed the gurdwaras, permitted themselves to be beaten, imprisoned, shot, maimed or burned alive with neither resistance nor complaint, and call on God…
May the whole Khalsa remember the wonderful Lord, and as it does so may it be blessed
May his protection be upon all members of the Khalsa wherever they may be.

FINDING OUT

❶ What is meant by 'initiation'?

❷ Why do you think the Amrit Ceremony is sometimes called Sikh baptism?

❸ Who can join the Khalsa? What does this tell us about Sikhism?

❹ Why are very young people not able to join the Khalsa? What do you think might be a suitable age to make a decision to join the Khalsa? Why?

❺ Why do you think five Sikhs lead the Amrit Ceremony (look back at Stimulus 1 for help)?

❻ What does sugar represent? What do you think this teaches about Sikhism?

❼ What do those initiated say before receiving the amrit? What do you think is the significance of what they say?

❽ Look at the extract from the prayers.
  (a) What were the glorious deeds of the five beloved ones (look at Stimulus 1 for help)?
  (b) How have Sikhs in the past shown their courage and loyalty?
  (c) What do Sikhs ask God to do for them?
  (d) How might this prayer help those Sikhs who have just been initiated?

stimulus 4 *Sikh identity*

> I am proud to be a Sikh and a member of the Khalsa. The day I joined the Khalsa was the most important day of my life so far. It was a sign I belonged to the Sikh community. It was like a new beginning for me. By wearing the five Ks, making promises about how to live my life and having the name Singh, I show everybody I am a loyal Sikh. The story of how the Khalsa was started inspires me. It teaches me that we should never be afraid to admit we are Sikhs.

Ravinder Singh (age 18)

The Sikh flag

Wearing the five ks and using the name Singh or Kaur identifies a person as a Sikh. Another important symbol of Sikh identity is the Nishan Sahib, the Sikh flag, which is found outside every Gurdwara (Sikh place or worship).

The Sikh flag

In the middle of the flag is the Sikh emblem, called the Khanda. This has three parts to it – the Khanda, two Kirpans and one Chakkha.

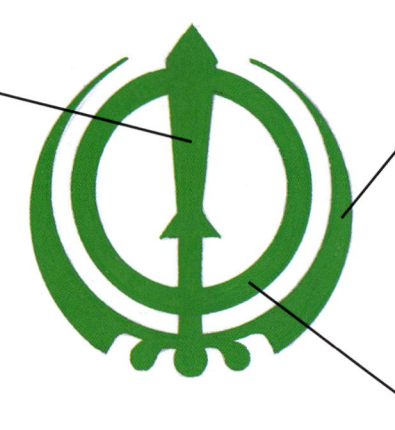

Khanda: A powerful weapon – a doubled-edged sword. The right edge represents freedom and authority; the left divine justice which punishes evil.

Two swords (Kirpans): The left sword represents God and spiritual things; the right represents the world and political power.

Chakkha: A circular shape. God, like a circle, has no beginning and no end. The Chakkha represents universal love and the oneness of humanity.

FINDING OUT

❶ How do you know Ravinder is male?

❷ Write down the three different ways Ravinder shows everybody he is a Sikh.

❸ Ravinder says that the day he joined the Khalsa was the most important day of his life and it was like a new beginning for him. What reasons might he give for saying this?

❹ Describe the Sikh flag in your own words. Describe its shape, its colour and the three parts of the emblem.

❺ Which part of the emblem represents freedom and justice?

❻ (a) Why is a circle used to represent God? (b) What else does the circle represent?

❼ There are two kirpans. What does each represent?

Thinking it over

❶ What does it mean to be loyal? How do people show loyalty?

❷ Should people always be loyal? Could being loyal to someone ever be wrong?

❸ The opposite of loyal is disloyal. What does this mean? Can you give an example?

❹ Is it important to belong to a group? Why/why not? Would you ever choose to be alone rather than be part of a group? Why? When? What is the difference between being alone and being lonely?

❺ Ravinder talks about not being afraid to admit he is a Sikh. Sometimes it isn't easy for people who belong to a group. Can you think of any examples of this? Why is it sometimes hard for people to belong to a particular group? What can be done to help people feel more comfortable about the groups they belong to?

MAKING CONNECTIONS

❶ Ravinder says he is proud to be a Sikh. What are you proud of?

❷ The story of how the Khalsa started inspires Ravinder. What does he mean? What has inspired you? How has it inspired you?

❸ Name a group you belong to. Why did you join? What do you enjoy about belonging to the group? What responsibilities do you have in the group?

❹ Some people display a flag in their gardens. People sometimes go to special events and take a flag with them to wave. Have you ever done this? Why do people do it? What does it say about their sense loyalty and belonging?

❺ Choose a flag you know, for example, the national flag or the Olympic flag. Draw it and explain what it represents.

❻ Can you think of a time when you have been loyal to someone? Who do you feel loyalty to?

❼ Think about the class you belong to. What's good about it? Do people get on? Do people look out for each other? What are its strengths and weaknesses? Devise a flag for your class which tries to represent its good points.

stimulus 5

Celebrating the Khalsa

Each year in April, usually on the 13th, Sikhs celebrate the festival of Baisakhi. This festival is a reminder of the beginning of the Khalsa.

Baisakhi is important because it remembers one of the most important days in Sikh history, when Guru Gobind Singh started off the Khalsa. In 1999, we celebrated the 300th anniversary of that event and we had a really great celebration. It is also important to me because in 1999 I was initiated into the Khalsa in the Amrit Ceremony. There were quite a few of us that year. It was a very emotional time for me. Another reason why it is important is because Baisakhi celebrates the culture of the Punjab. Sikhism began in the Punjab, and at Baisakhi we celebrate our music and cultural traditions of the Punjab. I think it is important to remember our roots. Although I was born in Glasgow, in some ways I think of the Punjab as my spiritual home. At Baisakhi we always have a procession which shows all the people in our community aspects of our Punjabi culture. We show people we are Sikhs and that being a Sikh is enjoyable.

How Baisakhi is celebrated

- The Sikh community attend the **Gurdwara**, the Sikh Temple, for special activities.
- New Khalsa members are initiated in the Amrit ceremony.
- It is customary at Baisakhi to hold elections to appoint the new committee which runs the gurdwara.

- The flagpole is lowered. The cloths around the flagpole and the Sikh flag are changed. The flagpole itself is washed with yoghurt, milk and water. After prayers have been said the flagpole is raised again.

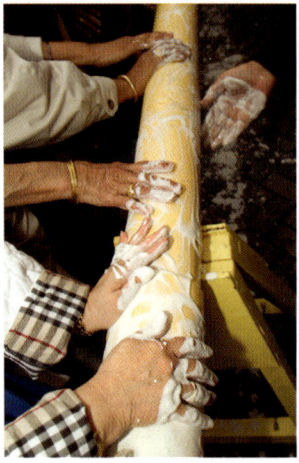

- In many Sikh communities there is a procession. Sikhs parade round the streets of their community, singing and chanting from the sacred writings, Guru Granth Sahib. At the front of the procession, the Guru Granth Sahib will be carried on a decorated float and all the members of the Sikh community will follow behind.

FINDING
OUT

❶ What does Baisakhi commemorate?

❷ When was the 300th anniversary of the formation of the Khalsa?

❸ Why would initiation into the Khalsa be an emotional time for a young Sikh?

❹ What do you think the writer means by referring to the Punjab as his 'spiritual home'?

❺ An important ritual at Baisakhi involves the flagpole. Describe the ritual. Give a reason why the flag and the flagpole are treated with such respect.

❻ In what ways might the celebration of Baisakhi enhance Punjabi culture?

Thinking it over

❶ Some events are so special that it is important to remember them every year. They should not be allowed to be forgotten. Do you agree with this statement? What events does it make you think of? Do you think a Sikh would say this about Baisakhi? Why/why not?

❷ Many Sikhs living in Britain today were born in Britain. Is it important that they remember the culture and traditions of the Punjab where their ancestors came from and where the Sikh religion began? Do you think Scots who have gone to live in other countries should keep Scottish traditions alive or should they follow the traditions of the country they live in?

6 A Sikh protest

THE DAILY NEWS

Sikhs protest French ban on headgear

Yesterday, thousands of Sikhs met to protest at the proposed ban on the wearing of religious symbols in French schools. Carrying placards and shouting slogans, Sikhs said that wearing turbans was an important part of their religion. The proposal means that the wearing of turbans will be banned. A spokesperson for the French government said its proposal would promote equality in schools, where all learners should be equal. The proposal has met with lots of criticism. A leading Scottish churchman said the ban would cause great distress to many who wished only to be loyal to their religion. A Sikh leader said, 'we feel undressed if we don't wear our turbans. Wearing a turban is part of our identity'. A Sikh teenager who has done all his schooling in France said, 'I will stop going to school. I will never take my turban off. I would feel naked without it.' The government spokesman said, 'Sikhs will be expected to obey the law like everyone else.'

1 Read the report in the *Daily News* and explain why Sikhs were protesting in France.

2 Why do Sikhs believe it is important to wear a turban?

3 The article says that Sikhs demonstrated with placards and by shouting slogans. Design a placard for the demonstration and make up a slogan.

4 What reason does the French government give for banning religious symbols in schools?

5 What reasons do Sikhs give for continuing to wear the turban?

6 In the 1970s there was a similar controversy in Britain. It had to do with Sikhs, turbans and motorbikes. Use your skills on the Internet to find out what this controversy was about. Write a paragraph explaining the controversy and what happened.

Thinking it over

1 What is your opinion about the controversy in France? Do you think Sikhs should be allowed to wear turbans in schools? Give reasons for your answer.

2 Why do some people find it difficult to accept people who are different from themselves? How do they show that they are not accepting them? Do you think acceptance is a good thing? Do you think we should always be tolerant? What makes you say that?

3 What kind of things should we not accept or tolerate? Should we ignore them or speak out against them?

4 Some Sikhs think the law about religious symbols is so bad they might decide to break it. Which do you think is more important – to accept the law of the land or follow religious teaching, even if it means breaking the law of the land? Can it ever be right to break the law of the land?

The Guru Granth Sahib

This section focuses on the Sikh sacred writings – the Guru Granth Sahib, also known as the Adi Granth. It begins by looking at a number of frequently asked questions relating to the importance of gurus within Sikhism. It considers the place of the Adi Granth in the gurdwara and describes two important traditions that take place there – the naming of a baby and the continuous reading of the Adi Granth, called an Akhand Path. It also looks at some important teachings on how Sikhs should live their lives.

IN THIS SECTION YOU WILL BE ASKED TO THINK ABOUT...

✓ Learning

✓ Respect

✓ Authority

✓ Selfishness

The Gurus – some frequently asked questions

> What does the word 'Sikh' mean?

Sikh means a disciple. A disciple is a learner. Sikhs learn about God and principles for living from their **Gurus**.

> The title 'Guru' is common in Sikhism. What does 'Guru' mean'?

The title 'Guru' means a teacher. It is a title of respect. The diagram shows how the word 'Guru' is made up from two words 'Gu' and 'Ru'.

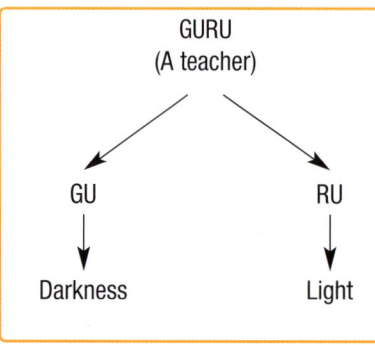

A Guru is a teacher who helps learners move from darkness to light, from ignorance to knowledge.

The first Guru was the founder of the Sikh religion – **Guru Nanak.** He lived about 500 years ago, from 1469–1539.

> Who was the first Guru?

> What did Guru Gobind Singh decide should be the next Guru?

Guru Gobind Singh decided the next Guru should be the Sikh Holy Book. He gave it the name the **Guru Granth Sahib**. It is also known as the Adi Granth.

- Guru means teacher.
- Granth means a collection of writings; Adi means first or original.
- Sahib is a title of respect like Lord or Sir.

> How many Gurus have there been?

There have been ten human Gurus. The last human Guru was Guru Gobind Singh. He lived about 300 years ago, from 1675–1708.

> What happened to Gurus when Guru Gobind Singh died?

> Why is the Guru Granth Sahib important to Sikhs?

Before he died, Guru Gobind Singh decided there should not be another human Guru. Human Gurus lived and they died. He decided that what Sikhs needed was a Guru who lived forever. Also there was a danger that if there was a human Guru he would be regarded as more important than all other Sikhs and Guru Gobind Singh thought this was not right. He believed everybody should be equal.

It is important because it is their Holy Book. This means it has authority over Sikhs. Like the human gurus, it teaches Sikhs about God and principles for living a good life. Sikhs try hard to put its teachings into practice.

❶ What does the word 'Sikh' mean?

❷ Explain why the word 'Guru' means a teacher.

❸ Explain why Guru Gobind Singh felt it was important to have a book as the next Guru and not a human guru.

❹ Work in groups of three or four to research one of the human Gurus. You will find information at www.sikhs.org. Produce a display headed 'The ten Sikh Gurus'.

❺ In the FAQs, dates are given for both Guru Nanak and Guru Gobind Singh. No dates are given for Guru Granth Sahib. Why do you think this is?

❻ Work with a partner and think of a question you could add to the FAQs. Discuss your questions with others in the class.

Thinking it over

❶ Guru means teacher. What makes a good teacher? Try to identify at least three things. Compare your answers with a partner.

❷ What do people mean when they say, 'ignorance is bliss'? Do you think it is true? Why/why not?

❸ What kinds of knowledge do you think 'religious' gurus are concerned with? Do you think they still have an important role to play today? What makes you say that?

❹ What's the best way for teachers and others to encourage you to do well?

stimulus 2 *Visiting a gurdwara*

MAKING CONNECTIONS

❶ A Guru is a teacher 'who helps learners move from ignorance to knowledge'. Write about a time when you learnt something that you thought was really important.

❷ Think of a book you have read which has influenced you in some way. How did it help you?

❸ Which is your preferred way of learning – reading a book, talking things through with others, or listening to the teacher? Why?

❹ Try to find examples of people who are referred to as 'gurus' because of their specialist knowledge, for example, in the worlds of business, education, self-help.

The Adi Granth should be opened each day for people to read but it should not be left open at night unless it is still being read.
   The Adi Granth should be opened, read and closed reverently. It should be placed in an elevated position on a stool in a clean place. It should be opened carefully. Small cushions should be used to support it and a rumala (square of cloth) used to cover it between reading whilst it is open. An awning (chanini) should be erected over the Adi Granth and a chauri (fan) should be available for waving over the Book.
   No book should be given the same reverence as the Adi Granth in the gurdwara and no secular event should be held there. The gurdwara may be used for any gathering whose purpose is the encouragement of religion. (Rehat Maryada)

A Sikh is showing some school students around her Gurdwara, the Sikh place of worship. Here are her notes for the visit.

Begin by explaining that the word 'gurdwara' means 'door of the Guru' and a building is a gurdwara if it contains the Guru Granth Sahib.

Ask pupils to take off their shoes and put a head covering on before entering Prayer Room. Tell pupils this is a sign of respect.

Joke about making sure they have put out their cigarettes. Explain it would not be showing respect to smoke in the presence of the Guru Granth Sahib.

Sit pupils down facing the Guru Granth Sahib and ask what they think the focal point of the prayer room is.

Distribute handout. Show and explain each feature on the hand out.

Point out that the Guru Granth Sahib is higher than sitting people because it is more important.

Ask why the area for the Guru Granth Sahib is like a throne – explain that the Guru Granth Sahib is a like a king or queen for Sikhs – it has authority over them.

Show rumalas – the special silk cloths which cover the Guru Granth Sahib when it is not being read.

Show the chauri – explain that it is waved over the Guru Granth Sahib as a sign of authority just as servants used to fan kings or queens in hot countries.

Explain that when Sikhs approach the Guru Granth Sahib they bow low and touch the ground with their foreheads and are careful not to turn their back on the Guru Granth Sahib. Explain this is a sign of respect.

Explain that a Granthi is a person who is trained to read the Guru Granth Sahib and has responsibility for looking after the Guru Granth Sahib. If a Granthi is present ask him to read an extract for pupils.

Explain that the Guru Granth Sahib is kept in a special room.

Explain that each day the Guru Granth Sahib is brought out in a procession and placed in the prayer hall, and then at night taken back to its resting place.

Explain that this is why most Sikhs don't have a copy of the Guru Granth Sahib at home, because it has to have its own room.

After questions take pupils down to kitchen for juice and biscuits

The throne room in a gurdwara

Bowing before the Guru Granth Sahib

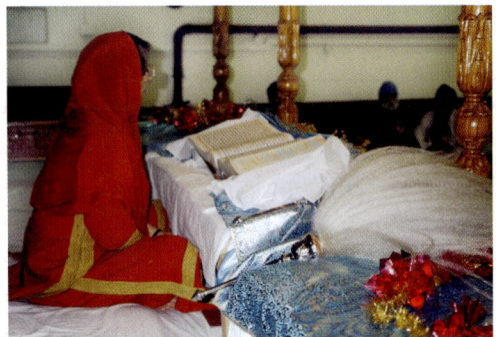

A Granthi reading from the Guru Granth Sahib

FINDING OUT

❶ What must a building contain before it can be regarded as a gurdwara?

❷ Copy the drawing of the throne room. Label on the drawing the canopy; the takht (raised platform); the manji (stool); the Guru Granth Sahib; the Granthi; the chauri.

❸ Explain why the Guru Granth Sahib is placed higher than the people sitting in the Gurdwara.

❹ What is a chauri and what is its importance for Sikhs?

❺ Explain why most Sikhs don't have a copy of the Guru Granth Sahib in their homes.

❻ List as many ways as you can in which Sikhs show respect for the Guru Granth Sahib.

❼ What is meant by the words 'reverence' and 'reverently'?

MAKING CONNECTIONS

❶ What does the word respect mean? Who or what do you respect? Why? How do you show your respect? Who respects you? How do they show that respect?

❷ Do you possess something which you insist has to be treated with respect? What is it? Why is it so special to you?

❸ Describe a situation when something that belonged to you or someone you know wasn't treated with respect? Say what happened and how people felt about it.

❹ The Guru Granth Sahib is the focal point of the prayer room. What does being 'the focal point' of something mean? What would you say is the focal point of your classroom? What is the focal point of your living room at home? Is it a good thing for a room to have a focal point? Why/why not?

Thinking it over

❶ What does 'showing respect for someone' mean? People won't respect you unless you respect them. Do you agree?

❷ People often say that respect has to be earned. What do they mean? How might you earn someone's respect?

❸ Is respect for people more important than respect for things? Give reasons for your answer.

❹ Some people argue that one of the problems in today's world is that not enough respect is shown. What evidence do they give for this point of view? Do you agree with them?

❺ 'Visiting religious buildings of different faiths and beliefs is a good idea.' Why might people say this? Do you agree?

stimulus 3 *Naming a Sikh baby*

From: Balbir@home.co.uk
To: Harjinderkaur124@aol.com

Subject: Baby Naming Ceremony
Attach: Jaswant.jpg
Hi Gran
Mum said I should e-mail you to thank you for the two presents you
sent. My baby sister will be pleased with the kara you sent. She'll
keep it for the rest of her life. I'm really pleased with the shirt
– it's a great pattern. Mum said I should tell you about the baby-
naming ceremony last Sunday. I've been to a few of them at the
gurdwara, but it's a bit special when it happens to your own family.
It's been funny the baby not having a name and by the time the
ceremony came round last Sunday she was ten days old – we've just
been calling her 'baby'. I have to admit when she cried in the middle
of the night I could think of a few other names to call her.

Anyway we all went to the gurdwara last Sunday morning, dressed in
our best – I put on my new shirt. Lots of people were there, all
wanting to have a look at the new baby. Then we came to the bit
where the name was going to be chosen. The Granthi opened the Guru
Granth Sahib at random and read out the passage on the top left-hand
page. After reading the passage, he announced the first letter of the
passage. It was the letter which sounded like 'j'. So we had to
choose a name beginning with the letter 'j'. Mum and Dad had been
thinking in advance about different names beginning with different
letters. They decided on Jaswant – so my baby sister is called
Jaswant Kaur. Jaswant means worthy of praise, and already she is
being praised. I prefer my name – Balbir – mighty and brave.

Some of my friends at school think it's an odd way of deciding on a
baby's name. I tell them it's a good way – our Holy Book guides and
helps us to choose a name. I ask my friends why they were given
their names – most of them have no idea. I tell them that the Guru
Granth Sahib is always present on special occasions and that when I
went to my Aunt's wedding she and her husband walked round the Guru
Granth Sahib four times as part of the ceremony.

Thanks again for the presents – hope you can
come and visit us soon and see your new
granddaughter. I've attached a photograph of
Jaswant. Who do you think she looks like?

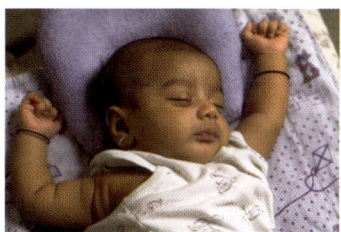

Lots of Love
Balbir

● Describe in your own words how Sikhs choose a name for a baby.

● What other special occasion does Balbir refer to where the Guru Granth Sahib is present? Carry out some research to find out more about this occasion.

● Jaswant was sent a kara. What is a kara and where it is worn? (See the section on the Khalsa.) Why do you think it was a good present to send the new baby?

● Balbir's Gran lives in the Punjab, which is where the Sikh religion began. Use an atlas to find out where the Punjab is.

● Carry out some research into the Punjab – collect information about its population, language, standard of living, currency, tourist attractions, main cities, religions.

MAKING CONNECTIONS

● The following reasons are often given why parents chose a particular name
  - The parents like it
  - The name is traditional in the family and had been used many times in the past
  - They named their child after somebody famous
  - For religious reasons

Find out why your parents chose your name. Can you think of any other reasons for choosing a name? What do you think is a good reason?

● What does your name mean? Does your name fit in with your personality?

● For Balbir, the naming ceremony was a special event in his family. What special events have been held in your family? Are they all connected with birth, marriage, death or have there been other special events. In what ways have these special, events helped you as a family?

stimulus 4 *An Akhand Path*

An important day in my life was last year when our Sikh community celebrated Guru Nanak's birthday. This is a very happy time when we remember the founder of our religion. One of the things we do at festivals, and also at times of joy and sorrow like births and deaths, is to read our Holy Book right through from beginning to end non stop. It isn't one person who does it. It's like a relay. We have a team of readers and we take it in turns to read a section. Last year was the first time I had taken part in it and I was dead nervous. My dad kept telling me to make sure I spoke out loud and clearly, and not too quickly. The Guru Granth Sahib has 1430 pages, so it takes about 48 hours to read the whole of the Guru Granth Sahib. As you can imagine it has to be well organised, so that when one person finishes a section, another one starts. I asked my mum why we do it and she said the custom began many years ago, before we had printed copies of the Guru Granth Sahib. There were so few copies of it, people read as much as they could before the Guru Granth Sahib was passed onto another group. We call this continuous reading an Akhand Path. Well I managed my part quite well – I read it very carefully and as clearly as I could. When I had finished everybody said how well I had done. I felt pretty pleased with myself.

Inderjit

1 Explain in your own words what an Akhand Path is.

2 On what occasions are they carried out?

3 What advice was Inderjit given about how to read her section?

4 Explain why the tradition of reading an Akhand Path began.

5 Find out as much as you can about the life of Guru Nanak and the origins of Sikhism.

MAKING CONNECTIONS

1 Write about a time when you had an important part to play in a celebration. What did you do? Was it successful? How did you feel?

2 If your class were asked to do a continuous reading of a book for charity, what would you choose? Why?

3 An Akhand Path is an important Sikh tradition. Can you think of any important traditions which are kept by your family or the community you belong to?

stimulus 5 Teachings from the Guru Granth Sahib

The Guru Granth Sahib expresses Sikh beliefs about God, and is also an authoritative guide for Sikhs on how they should live. Sikhs aim to live God-centred lives (Gurmukh) rather than lives which are motivated by selfish desires (Manmukh). To become Gurmukh, Sikhs should do good and avoid evil. The following teachings from the Guru Granth Sahib give advice on how Sikhs should live their lives.

1 Unhappy is he who lives under the influence of greed.

2 Give up bad actions and only do good actions.

3 Do not be angry with any person.

4 He is brave who fights for the downtrodden.

5 Shame to him who commits adultery.

6 Recognise your master, and have sympathy for others.

7 Son, why do you quarrel with your father? It is a sin to argue with him.

8 If I have committed theft and gained something, I have gained dishonour in this world and the next.

9 Those who torment the poor are in turn tormented by the Lord.

10 Whosoever is kind to others, the Lord receives him with kindness.

11 A life devoid of love is a flower blooming in the wilderness, with nobody to enjoy its fragrance.

12 Do not be cruel to any creature.

13 One should practise truth, contentment and mercy.

FINDING OUT

① What is meant by Gurmukh and Manmukh?

② Work in pairs. Look carefully at the 13 teachings. Decide what is the main point of each, and whether the action or quality described is Gurmukh or Manmukh. Complete the table below for each teaching. The first two are done for you.

Teaching	Gurmukh (God-centred)	Manmukh (Self-centred)
Teaching 1		Being greedy
Teaching 2	Doing good actions	
Teaching 3		

③ In groups choose one of the teachings and discuss ideas for a short story or drama that illustrates it.

④ In groups look at the drawings which accompany the teachings. Choose one other teaching and discuss ideas for your own group drawing.

⑤ What do you think is meant by 'an authoritative guide' for Sikhs on how they should live?

⑥ What is the difference between 'authoritative' and 'authoritarian'?

⑦ What do you think is meant by 'self-centred'? Is being self-centred the same as being 'selfish'?

MAKING CONNECTIONS

① Describe the kind of 'authority' that each of the following has over you?
- a doctor
- a politician
- the police
- a teacher
- parents
- a court of law

❷ Do you have 'authority' over anyone? Describe what it involves.

❸ Who has the greatest authority over you? Are you happy about that? Why/why not?

❹ Look at the actions/qualities that you placed under 'Manmukh' in question 2 of *Finding out*. Which ones would you say you do in your own life?

❺ Do you know anyone who is self-centred? Can you give examples of their self-centred behaviour?

❻ Describe an occasion when you acted selfishly. How did you feel afterwards? What might you want to change about yourself in order to become less selfish?

❼ Look at the actions/qualities that you placed under Gurmukh in question 2 of *Finding out*. Which ones would you say you do in your own life?

❽ Do you agree that most of us are capable of doing good things – we are kind, thoughtful and generous but we are also capable of being mean, selfish and thoughtless. Why is this?

Thinking it over

❶ The Guru Granth Sahib encourages Sikhs to think about what sort of person they want to be. Is it important that people do this? Why/why not?

❷ 'Nobody and nothing should tell us what to do and how to behave. We should decide for ourselves.' What might be the advantages and disadvantages of following such a principle?

❸ Why do you think some people are self-centred and selfish? Do you think people who are selfish can become unselfish? What needs to happen?

❹ What is meant by 'looking after number one'? What might be the advantages and disadvantages of following this principle?

❺ Do you think authority should always be obeyed? Or are there times when you should resist authority? Can you give examples? Is it important to be aware of the consequences of resisting authority? Why?

❻ How do you define goodness? How do we know what is good and what is not good?

❼ 'Even if you are not a Sikh the Guru Granth Sahib can be worth reading and learning from.' Do you agree? Give reasons for your answer.

Mool Mantra

The Sikh teaching about God is contained in the Mool Mantra. This unit looks at the basic teachings of the Mool Mantra. It describes ways in which Sikhs are encouraged to think about and remember God, and considers what their sacred writings and stories teach about God.

IN THIS SECTION YOU WILL BE ASKED TO THINK ABOUT...

✓ Influences on your life

✓ God

✓ Religious language

stimulus 1 Beliefs about God and influences on life

3. I don't believe in God. There is no evidence for God. People who believe in God say He made the world. What I want to know is – if God made the world who made God?

1. I believe in a higher power which is behind the universe. If more people believed in this power, it would make the world a better place and people better human beings.

2. Sometimes I think God exists – there must be a reason why human beings are on earth, but sometimes I'm not sure. I wish there was proof God exists but there isn't.

4. I have been brought up to believe in God. I go to the Gurdwara regularly. Believing in God is the most important thing in my life.

5. I think love is the most important thing in life. What people need is love, not belief in God.

A person who believes in God is known as a **theist**.

A person who does not believe in God is known as an **atheist**.

A person who is not sure about whether God exists or not is known as an **agnostic**.

In a poll conducted for a BBC programme 10,000 people were asked who or what has influenced their lives most. The results were as follows:

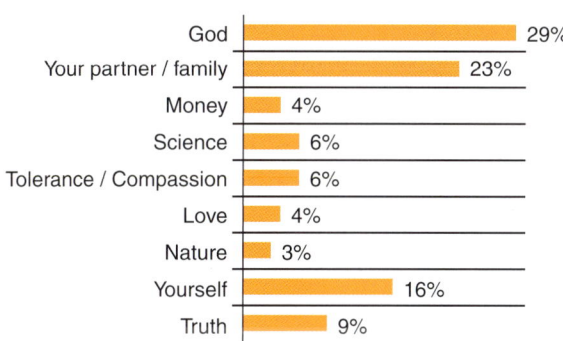

Who or what is most influential in your life?

God	29%
Your partner / family	23%
Money	4%
Science	6%
Tolerance / Compassion	6%
Love	4%
Nature	3%
Yourself	16%
Truth	9%

SOURCE: BBC

FINDING OUT

❶ For each viewpoint decide whether it was said by a theist, an atheist or an agnostic.

❷ A Sikh said one of the viewpoints. Which one? How do you know?

❸ Viewpoint 1 talks about God as a higher power. Using that as a starting point, and working with a partner, brainstorm what people mean when they talk about God. Share your ideas in a class discussion. Produce a class display headed 'What people mean by God'.

❹ What reason is given in viewpoint 2 for the existence of God?

❺ Explain in your own words the reason given in viewpoint 3 for not believing in God.

❻ People were surveyed to find out what 'influences' them most in life. What is meant by 'influences'?

❼ According to the survey results, what are the three most and the three least important influences in life?

❽ Look at viewpoint 1 in stimulus 1. How does this person think belief in God influences people?

MAKING CONNECTIONS

❶ Which of the five viewpoints in stimulus 1 is nearest your own view about God? Why?

❷ If you were asked to respond to the survey which three would have been your most important influences and which three your least? Compare your results with a partner.

❸ Divide the class into eight groups. Four groups should devise a simple questionnaire to hand out to family, friends, or students in other classes to find out their beliefs about God. Are people theists, atheists or agnostics and what is their understanding of God? The other four groups should find out who or what has influenced people most in their lives and how those things have influenced them. Each group should then report their findings to the other groups.

Thinking it over

❶ Some people argue that the most important influence in the lives of teenagers is their friends. Do you agree? Why/why not?

❷ Do you think newspapers and television have too much influence on people's views and attitudes? What makes you say that?

❸ Do you think people should be more questioning about what they read in newspapers and hear on television? What kind of questions should they ask?

❹ There is a famous song entitled '*I did it my way*'. Do you think this is a useful principle to live your life by? Why/why not?

❺ Do you think it is possible to prove God exists? Is it reasonable to believe in things that cannot be proved? Can you give any examples?

❻ What does the word 'God' mean to you? Do you believe in God? Give reasons for your opinion.

stimulus 2 *The Mool Mantra*

There is one God,
Whose name is truth
Creator of all things and the all-pervading spirit
Fearless and without hatred
Timeless and formless
Beyond birth and beyond death
Self enlightened
By the grace of the Guru is God known

The Mool Mantra in Gurmukhi script (left) and translated into English (right)

Mool means 'basic' and Mantra means 'saying'. The Mool Mantra is the basic statement of belief about God for Sikhs, teaching Sikhs what God is like.

The Mool Mantra is poetry. It was written by the founder of the Sikh religion, Guru Nanak, and can be found at the beginning of the Holy Book, the Guru Granth Sahib.

The Mool Mantra is written in the Gurmukhi language. Gurmukhi means 'from the mouth of the Gurus'.

The Mool Mantra refers to God in gender-free language, though in some translations God is sometimes referred to as Him.

1 Who wrote the Mool Mantra? What do the words 'Mool Mantra' mean?

2 In what language is the the Mool Mantra written?

3 Have a class discussion to compare ideas about what each line of the Mool Mantra means.

4 Write out each line of the Mool Mantra onto a separate card. Look at the statements below. Copy each statement onto a separate card. Match each of the cards of the Mool Mantra to a statement card.
- God **creates** everything in the world
- God is not like humans. Humans are frightened of things like pain and death. Humans are capable of hatred. God is without **fear**. God is without **hate**.
- Sikhs believe there is only **one** God.
- God is not like humans. Humans need others to learn. God doesn't need anybody but him/her**self**.
- All things that are true come from God. God is **truth**.

- God is not like humans. Humans live only a little time and then they die. They live in a body and are limited by what their body allows them to do. God is not limited by **time** and God does not have a physical **form**.
- God is generous to humans because through the teaching of great teachers and the holy book, God allows humans to **know** something about God.
- God is not like humans. Humans are born, live and die. There is no **birth** or **death** for God. God is forever.

5 In Sikhism is God thought of as male or female or both?

6 Ask your teacher to show you a copy of the Mool Mantra. Working in pairs, pick out all the words and phrases you find difficult to understand. Discuss in class what they mean. Remember each line is saying something about God.

7 Write a short paragraph headed 'What Sikhs believe about God'. Display class answers next to the earlier display 'What people believe about God'. Do you notice any similarities or differences?

8 Look at the completed crossword below. Make up clues for each of the answers. There are 4 answers across and 4 down. Use the information in Stimulus 4 and your knowledge of Sikhism from the other units you have studied to help you.

stimulus

3 *Thinking about God*

From a very young age Sikh children will be taught the Mool Mantra and learn to say it as a prayer. They will hear it at home and in the gurdwara (place of worship). For Sikhs it is important to focus on God everyday. This stimulus shows some of the ways Sikhs do this.

> Those who meditate on God do good to others. (Guru Granth Sahib

> A Sikh should rise early, take a bath and then meditate on the one true God. (Rehat Maryada)

> The individual Sikh should be constant in studying the scriptures and meditating upon God. (Rehat Maryada)

This symbol is called the 'Ik Onkar' symbol. It is the opening words of the Mool Mantra – 'There is only one God'. The Ik Onkar symbol is important for Sikhs because these words express an important belief. Some Sikhs display the symbol in their homes and the symbol can be found in the gurdwara and on rumalas (a special cloth used in the gurdwara). Sometimes it is used as a lapel badge.

> Holy congregation is the school of the true Guru. There we learn to love God and appreciate his greatness. (Guru Granth Sahib)

Some Sikhs use a rosary or mala as a way of helping them to concentrate when they are meditating. It is usually made of wool with 108 knots or beads on it.

Often when Sikhs meditate they will say over and over again the word 'Waheguru'. This name means 'Wonderful Lord'. Praying everyday is a way of helping Sikhs to focus on God.

Although prayers to God can be offered by Sikhs at any time and any place, they must also be offered in public along with other members of the Sikh community in the Gurdwara.

Sunday is the day when most Sikhs will go with their families to the gurdwara. The service starts with readings from the sacred writings. A large part of the Sikh sacred writings is in poetry which has been set to music, and the singing of these verses to the accompaniment of musical instruments is the main feature of Sikh congregational worship.

Here are some of the words used in prayer when Sikhs meet together for worship.

O true King and loving Father, we have sung your sweet hymns, heard your word which gives life and talked of your many blessings. May these find a place in our hearts so that our souls may be drawn towards you.

O Father, save us from lust, anger, greed, worldly attachment and pride.

O kind and living Father…grant that we may be obedient to your will.

FINDING OUT

❶ How should a Sikh begin each day?

❷ What is meditation?

❸ What according to the Guru Granth Sahib will be the result of meditation?

❹ What does it mean to say a 'Sikh should be constant in studying the Scriptures'?

❺ What is a 'mala' and how might it help Sikhs with meditation?

❻ What name for God do Sikhs repeat over and over again to help them remember God? What does this name mean? What does it teach about how Sikhs think of God?

❼ Draw the Ik Onkar symbol. What is a symbol? When Sikhs sees the Ik Onkar symbol what does it remind them of?

❽ What do you think is meant by 'Holy congregation is the school of the true guru'?

❾ According to the prayer what is God like?

❿ In the prayer Sikhs ask God to save them from 'worldly attachment'. What is meant by worldly attachment?

MAKING CONNECTIONS

❶ Describe your routine from the time you get up in the morning until you leave for school. Are you satisfied with your routine or do you think it needs changing in any way? For example, do you need to get up earlier to give yourself more time?

❷ Do you find it difficult to concentrate sometimes? Why do you think that is? What do you think you can do about this? Do you think some form of meditation might help?

❸ Some Sikhs use prayer beads to help them concentrate when thinking about God. Do you know any other religious groups who use prayer beads? How and why do they use them?

❹ The Ik Onkar symbol can be used as a badge. What is the purpose of a badge? Have you ever worn a badge? What did it represent? Draw up a list of badges that people in the class have worn or know about. Is it possible to classify them into different types?

❺ Look at the two badges below. Write down what each badge tells you about the people who wear it.

 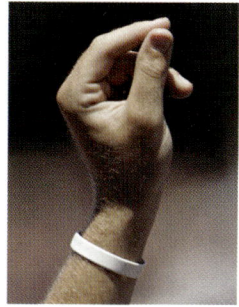

❻ Look again at the prayer said during Sikh worship. What do Sikhs ask God to save them from? What might you ask God to save you from and why?

4 Sikh belief in God

Story 1

Guru Nanak, the founder of the Sikh religion, travelled to many different places, including holy places in different religions. Once he was in Makkah visiting the Ka'aba which is a holy place for Muslims. After his long journey he was very tired and fell asleep with his feet pointing towards the holy shrine. Some people were very angry at this. They said he was being disrespectful to God. Guru Nanak apologised but then asked them if they could lay him down and point his feet in a direction where God is not.

Story 2

A holy man got up one morning. He bathed and meditated, thinking about God. Then he thought I'll have something to eat and I'll find somebody to share my food with. He walked through the village but nobody wanted to share his food. Eventually he came across an old man who looked hungry. He asked him if he wanted to come to his house to eat. The old man agreed.

The holy man brought out the food. 'Before we eat,' he said, 'we must remember God and repeat his name.' The old man became very angry at this. He said, 'what has God done for me? Nothing – I'll never repeat his name,' and he began to swear and curse God's name. The holy man was very upset at this and threw him out of his house.

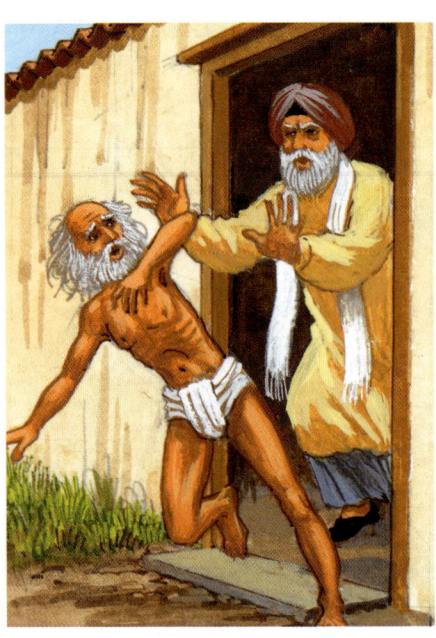

To calm down the holy man decided to meditate. While meditating he heard a voice. It was God. 'What have you done?' God said. 'Why have you thrown the man out of your house? The holy man replied, 'because he was showing disrespect to You.' God replied, 'you decided to share your food in my name but instead you threw him out in my name. I have listened to that man for 75 years but I still give him the gift of a new day everyday; he is my son and I love him. You listen to him for ten minutes and throw him out!'

God is like sugar scattered in the sand. An elephant cannot pick it up... Become an ant and partake of it. (Guru Granth Sahib)

Why do you go to the forest to find God? He lives in all and yet remains detached. He dwells in you as well, as fragrance resides in a flower or the reflection in a mirror. God lives in everything. See him, therefore, in your heart. (Guru Granth Sahib)

FINDING OUT

❶ Why were people angry with Guru Nanak?

❷ What point was Guru Nanak trying to make?

❸ What does the first story teach Sikhs about God? Give the story a title.

❹ Why did the holy man become angry at the old man and how did he show his anger?

❺ According to the story what was God's reaction to what the holy man had done?

❻ What does the second story teach Sikhs about God? Give the story a title.

❼ Work in pairs. One should tell the story from the point of view of the holy man and the other from the old man. In each case think about the feelings of each character and the reasons why he acted the way he did. Compare versions. How do they differ?

❽ What do you think is meant by the following:
a) God is like sugar scattered in the sand.
b) God lives in people 'as fragrance resides in a flower or the reflection in a mirror'?

Thinking it over

❶ 'It's raining cats and dogs' is an example of symbolic or metaphorical language. What is meant by describing some language as symbolic or metaphorical? Can you give another example?

❷ In which of the following kinds of writing would you expect to find symbolic and metaphorical language? Explain your choices.
   a) A newspaper report of an accident.
   b) A contract detailing the sale of a house.
   c) A poem.
   d) A letter to a solicitor.
   e) A novel.

❸ If a story is symbolic or metaphorical does this mean it is not true?

❹ What makes a story true or not true?

❺ Is a poem true or not true?

❻ Why do you think language about God is often symbolic and metaphorical?

❼ Where is God? 'God lives in everything'. (Gura Granth Sahib) Do you agree with this statement? Explain your answer.

❽ In this section you have studied Sikh beliefs about God. State three things you have learned. Have your views on what God could be like and whether God exists or not changed in any way?

Langar

The Langar is an important feature of a gurdwara. The word 'langar' means 'a free kitchen'. This unit introduces some of the practices associated with the langar and the beliefs and values which lie behind it. It looks at the Sikh teaching about equality and explores some Sikh stories. It also considers the work of Sikhs in relation to human rights.

IN THIS SECTION YOU WILL BE ASKED TO THINK ABOUT...

✓ Humility
✓ Equality
✓ Service
✓ Difference
✓ Rights

stimulus **1**

The langar

A langar at a Gurdwara

Michael Palin describes his visit to the langar at the Golden Temple in Amritsar.

All Sikh temples have a langar, a kitchen preparing free meals round the clock, financed through the one-tenth of their income all Sikhs are expected to give to good works. It's a huge operation, with an estimated 50,000 meals prepared each weekday and twice that at weekends. The work is all done by volunteers, and any Sikh, whether surgeon or street cleaner is expected to come and help chop onions or wash dishes. In the words of one of the ten holy Gurus on whose teachings Sikhism is based, 'if you want to understand me, come into my kitchen'.

The kitchen is spread through several buildings. One is entirely devoted to a chapatti production line. Flour is fed into a slowly turning machine, which regurgitates the flour as dough. One group of helpers rolls the dough into balls, another flattens each ball into a pancake, and another lays them out on hotplates capable of taking a couple of hundred chappatis at a time. The chappati production line shares a tall barn-like space with dal cauldrons, the largest cooking vessels I've ever seen.

I pick my way through the kitchens, across a terrace where 30–40 people sit slicing onions and garlic, green peppers and ginger, and up the stairs to take a meal in one of the spartan communal dining rooms. Volunteers pass through, giving out segmented steel trays, which others then fill up with chapatti, dollops of pickle and dal ladled out of steel buckets. Water is poured into our mugs from another basket.

As a helpful man next to me says, this whole process embodies the Sikh teaching that we are all equal and we must learn to serve each other.

(*Himalaya* by Michael Palin, Orion)

❶ What are dal and chappatis?

❷ Describe what was happening in the kitchens.

❸ Who is expected to volunteer to work in the langar?

❹ 'If you want to understand me, come into my kitchen.' What do you think is meant by this?

❺ Match each of the following values to one of the sentences below:

equality; hospitality; service; humility.

- Sikhs believe it is important to make visitors feel welcome.
- Everybody is at the langar regardless of their gender, religion, or country of origin.
- Sikhs usually take turns to help in the langar – nobody is too important to avoid doing it.
- Sikhs believe they should spend time working in the langar, preparing, giving out the food and clearing up.

❻ Find phrases in the account which show that:

a) Michael Palin was made welcome.
b) all Sikhs should help – nobody's too important.

❼ Design a poster which welcomes people to the langar no matter what their social position, wealth, religion, nationality is.

❽ Where is Amritsar?

❾ Find out when the Golden Temple was built and by which Guru. How did it get its name?

MAKING CONNECTIONS

1 Are you a vegetarian? Do you know anyone who is? How strict are they?

2 Sikhs give their time voluntarily to help in the langar. Describe a time when you have given your time to do voluntary work.

3 Describe a situation when someone has shown humility.

4 Describe an occasion when you have had to welcome people to an event or party. What kind of things did you do to welcome them? Do you think you were successful? How do you know?

5 The opposite of humility is arrogance. Do you know any people who behave in an arrogant way? How do they behave? Have you ever behaved in an arrogant way? What happened? How did you feel afterwards?

4 The Sikh word for service is 'sewa'. What is service? Do you think the Sikh idea of expecting people in important positions to serve in the langar is a good one? Why?

5 Write an acrostic poem entitled 'Sewa'.

stimulus 2 *Sikh teaching about equality*

Distributing karah parshad

A Symbol of Equality

Karah parshad is a sweet food made from plain flour, unsalted butter (ghee), sugar, semolina and water mixed into a paste. As it is prepared hymns are usually sung. When it is ready it is blessed and given to everyone present at the gurdwara. Karah parshad is also distributed on a special occasion such as a wedding or a name-giving ceremony. According to the Rehat Maryada there is to be no favouritism or greed when distributing or receiving karah parshad. It involves an act of sharing and is a symbol of equality.

Thinking it over

1 Although some Sikhs are not vegetarian, it is always vegetarian food which is served in the langar. Why do you think this is? What are the arguments in favour of vegetarianism? Are you convinced by them? Why or why not?

2 Giving time as a volunteer is actually harder than giving money to charity. Do you agree or disagree? Why?

3 'The winner showed humility.' How might someone who is a 'winner' show humility? Can you give an example? Is someone who shows humility to be admired? Why/why not? Is it difficult sometimes to show humility? What makes you say that?

> Every Sunday morning I attend my local gurdwara for worship with many other Sikhs. We all sit on the floor, women on one side and men on another. Towards the end of our worship a sweet warm mixture called karah parshad is distributed to all Sikhs present, and then eaten. Its sweetness represents God's goodness and eating it together is a symbol that all present are equal members of the Sikh community. Nobody is better than anybody else. After worship is over we go to the langar to eat a meal together.

Mohan Singh

Religions consist not of mere worship, he who looks on all as equal is religious. (Guru Nanak)

From the Divine Light the whole creation sprang, why then should we divide creatures into high and low. (The Guru Granth Sahib)

A gurdwara is open to anyone regardless of caste or creed (beliefs). (Rehat Maryada)

Sitting on special cushions, chairs, couches or sofas or in any way demonstrating social distinction or superiority is deemed contrary to Sikhism. (Rehat Maryada)

In the congregation there should be no distinction of social status or caste or between Sikh and non-Sikh. (Rehat Maryada)

 **FINDING OUT**

1. What is karah parshad? What ingredients is it made from?

2. According to the Rehat Maryada what is forbidden when distributing or receiving karah parshad?

3. According to Mohan Singh what does the eating of karah parshad symbolise?

4. Sikhs say making and sharing karah parshad is more than eating food, it is an act of worship. What do you think they mean when they say this?

5. Working in groups, discuss the five quotations and come to a conclusion about what they mean. Be prepared to report back to the whole class.

MAKING CONNECTIONS

1. At worship Sikhs share karah parshad. What examples from other religions do you know where people share food at worship?

2. Sharing food and eating together can make people feel they belong. Describe a time when enjoying food together in a group has made you feel you belong.

3. Can you think of places or situations today where there is inequality: between men and women; between rich and poor; between religions; between ethnic groups?

4. Look at the five quotations of Sikh teaching again. Is there one which you think is especially important? Explain why you chose it. Design a banner to illustrate the saying.

Thinking it over

1 What kind of things are people arguing for when they say they want equality?

2 Are any two people ever really equal? In what ways can people be said to be equal?

3 Does everyone deserve to be treated equally? Can you think of any reasons why someone should not be treated equally?

4 Does treating people equally mean that everybody should be treated in exactly the same way? What makes you say that?

5 What is meant by 'equality of opportunity'? Is it possible to give everyone the same opportunities? What kind of opportunities do you think everyone should have?

6 'Nobody is better than anybody else' says Mohan Singh. What do you think she means? Do you agree or disagree? Why?

stimulus
3 Sikh stories

The first story comes from a time when Sikhs were being persecuted and were involved in fighting for their faith.

At the end of one day's particularly fierce fighting, a Sikh soldier called Bhai Kanahya came at out onto the battlefield looking for wounded soldiers. He was carrying a bottle of water and gave the water to anyone who needed it. When his fellow Sikh soldiers saw what he was doing they were furious, because

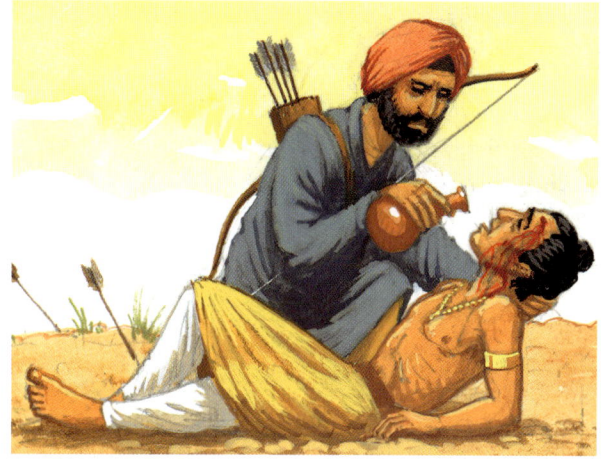

he was offering water not only to the Sikh soldiers, but also the enemy soldiers. He was summoned to see the Guru. Guru Gobind Singh asked him what he was doing, and why he was giving water to enemy soldiers. He replied, 'I see only human beings who need water and comfort, I do not see enemy soldiers.'

———————————

One day Guru Amar Das (the third human Guru) was visited by the Muslim Emperor, a very important and powerful person. Instead of being given special treatment and taken to the Guru straight away, he was asked, like everybody else, to sit on the ground with all the other visitors. He was told that the rule of the Guru was 'first eat together then meet together'.

❶ In the first story how did Bhai Kanahya treat the enemy soldiers?

❷ Why do you think his fellow Sikh soldiers were furious at what he did?

❸ 'Bhai' means brother. What does this story teach about who Bhai Kanahya thought was his brother?

❹ 'I see only human beings who need water and comfort, I do not see enemy soldiers.' What do you think Bhai Kanahya meant by this?

❺ Give the first story a title.

❻ In the second story what was the Emperor asked to do when he arrived? Do you think he would have been expecting to be greeted in this way? Why not?

❼ How does this story show Sikh belief about equality?

Thinking it over

❶ 'The best way to destroy enemies is to make them your friend.' Do you agree?

❷ Would you agree that some people can be frightened of others who are different from them? Can you give an example? What do you think they can do about this?

❸ 'First eat together then meet together.' Do you agree that this could be a helpful rule to follow when faced with people who are different? Why/why not?

 **4** *Sikhism and human rights*

A story about Guru Nanak

One day, as was his custom, Nanak went to the river early in the morning to bathe. However, he failed to return to the village. His clothes were found on the river bank. Everyone was convinced he had drowned. They dragged the river but no body was discovered.

Three days later Nanak reappeared. Naturally everybody was curious, but Nanak remained silent. The next day he spoke and said 'There is neither Hindu nor Muslim, so whose path shall I follow? I shall follow God's path. God is neither Hindu nor Muslim and the path which I follow is God's'. From that day on Nanak began to teach and spread God's message. Everybody is equal. God loves everybody, no matter how they worship him. Guru Nanak believed that the outward differences between religions were not important and what was more important was how people lived their lives and treated others.

Extract from the United Nations Declaration of Human Rights (1948)

All human beings are born free and equal.
Everyone has the right to life, liberty and security of person.
No one should be subjected to torture.
Everyone has the right to freedom of movement.
Everyone has the right to freedom of thought, conscience and opinion.
Everyone has the right to a standard of living adequate for the health and well-being of himself and of his family, including food, clothing, housing and medical care.

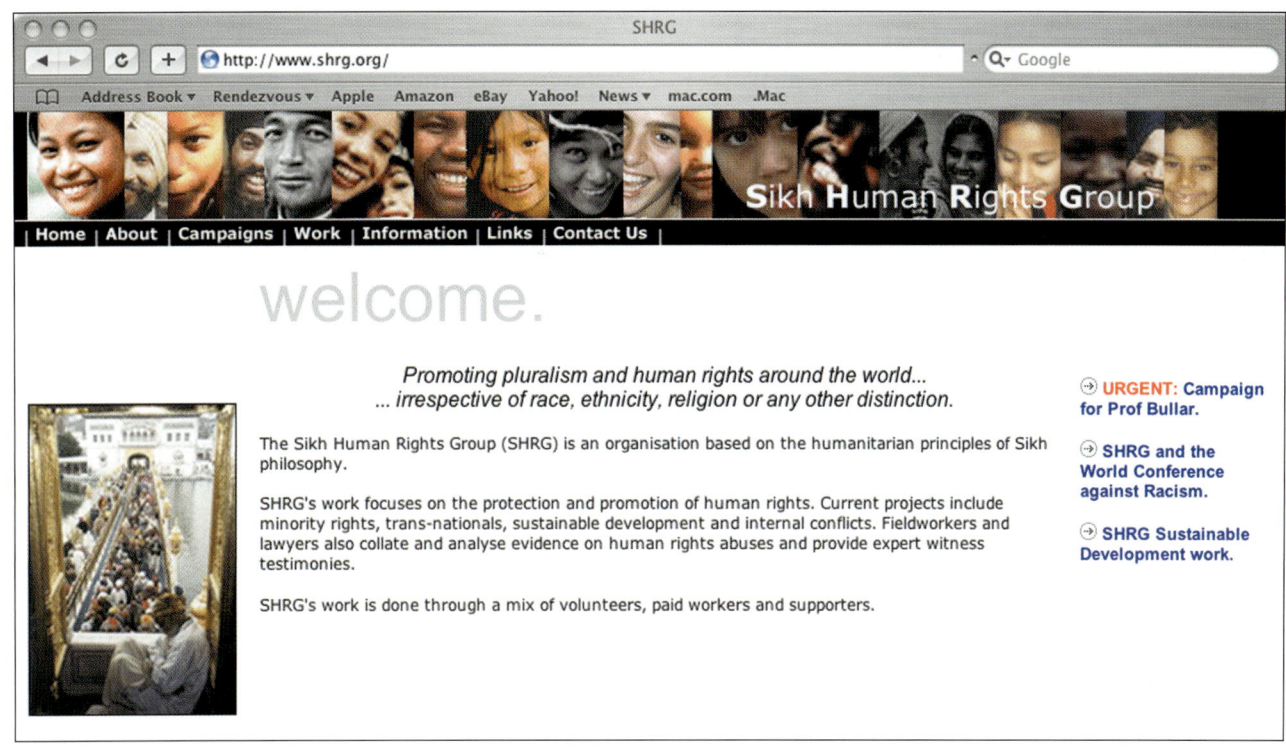

| Home | About | Campaigns | Work | Information | Links | Contact Us |

welcome.

Promoting pluralism and human rights around the world...
... irrespective of race, ethnicity, religion or any other distinction.

The Sikh Human Rights Group (SHRG) is an organisation based on the humanitarian principles of Sikh philosophy.

SHRG's work focuses on the protection and promotion of human rights. Current projects include minority rights, trans-nationals, sustainable development and internal conflicts. Fieldworkers and lawyers also collate and analyse evidence on human rights abuses and provide expert witness testimonies.

SHRG's work is done through a mix of volunteers, paid workers and supporters.

→ **URGENT: Campaign for Prof Bullar.**

→ **SHRG and the World Conference against Racism.**

→ **SHRG Sustainable Development work.**

 **FINDING OUT**

❶ Explain what is meant in the story when Nanak says ' There is neither Hindu nor Muslim'?

❷ What are human rights?

❸ Read the extract from the declaration of Human Rights. Make a list of the rights it says all human beings should have. Underline any you are not sure what it means and discuss in class its meaning

❹ Choose one of the rights and describe a situation you know about, where this 'right' is being ignored.

❺ Look at the screenshot of the website. What do the letters SHRG stand for?

❻ Discuss in class what SHRG aims to do and how they do it. Write a paragraph explaining what they do.

❼ Look at the photographs at the top of the screenshot. How do they show that the SHRG fights for rights for all people and not just Sikhs?

Thinking it over

1 How important is it to have a statement of human rights? Does it guarantee that people's human rights will be respected? Why do you think human rights are sometimes ignored despite the United Nations Declaration?

2 Do all human beings have the same rights? Do human beings always have these rights? Can they be taken away? Do people who have committed serious crimes have human rights? Why/why not?

3 Should governments always uphold human rights? Are there circumstances when they should ignore certain human rights? Choose one of the rights from the United Nations list and argue your case for or against.

4 The declaration of human rights begins 'All humans are born free and equal'. If humans are born free and equal, what goes wrong? Whose fault is it that the world is not an equal place?

5 'Outward differences between religions are not important. What is more important is how people live their lives and treat others'. Why do some people think that the differences between religions are important? What do you think?

6 Look at the 7 statements below. Think about what each means. Which do you agree with? Which do you disagree with? Why? Compare your answer with a partner.

> People in Britain today take human rights for granted. They forget about those who don't have them.

> Organisations like SHRG are just wasting their time – there'll never be human rights and a fair deal for everybody.

> It's no good moaning about unfairness and injustice if you don't do anything about it.

> If you are religious, fighting injustice is more important than going to a religious building to worship.

> Making sure people have equal rights is more important than making sure people have enough to eat.

> Even terrorists and people who have committed serious crimes have human rights.

> There is too much talk about human rights, what is more important is human responsibility.

MAKING CONNECTIONS

1 Write down as many statements as you can to complete the phrase, 'It's not fair that...' which relate to your own experience of life and your knowledge of what goes on in the world.

2 Produce a class list of 10 'It's not fair statements'. Put them in order of unfairness. For each one, discuss who is to blame for the unfairness and what might be done to put the situation right.

3 The work of SHRG depends on paid workers and volunteers. Would you consider being a paid worker or a volunteer for an organisation which fights for human rights? What qualities and skills do you think you would need?

4 Have you ever signed a petition or gone on a demonstration to protest about injustice and unfairness? What was the reason?

5 Choose one issue which you think illustrates injustice. Write a letter to your MP or MSP explaining why you think there is injustice.

6 What other organisations do you know about which fight for human rights? You might find www.amnesty.org.uk useful.

Vand Chhakna

Vand Chhakna is the Sikh belief about the importance of sharing one's earnings. This section introduces Sikh teaching on wealth and explores some stories about wealth associated with Guru Nanak. It also introduces Kirat Karna, the Sikh principle of earning one's living by honest means. The section describes the work of Pingalwara, a Sikh organisation founded on the principle of sewa or service to others.

IN THIS SECTION YOU WILL BE ASKED TO THINK ABOUT...

✓ Wealth

✓ Honesty

✓ Work

✓ Success

stimulus 1

Sikh teaching about wealth

One day Guru Nanak went to stay at the house of a rich merchant. He arrived on the day the merchant was holding a great feast. As Guru Nanak came near the house he saw that there were many, many flags flying outside the house. He asked the merchant why this was and was told that the flags represented how much money he had. Each flag represented 1,000 rupees. The merchant was obviously very rich.

Later that day, during the feast Guru Nanak went up to the merchant and asked him if the merchant would do him a favour. The merchant agreed and Guru Nanak asked him to look after a needle for him and to take good care of it, because in the next life after he died, he would ask for it back. This puzzled the merchant. Eventually he realised that he would never be able to give Guru Nanak the needle back in the next life, because you can't take anything with you when you die. The Guru was trying to teach him a lesson. If he couldn't take a tiny needle into the next life, what was the good of all his wealth?

Sikh teaching about money

1 Blessed is the godly person and the riches they possess because they can be used for charitable purposes.
2 He who labours hard, earns honestly and gives something in charity has found the Path of Truth.
3 A gambler suffers much anxiety.
4 Sikhs should voluntarily set aside a tenth of their income to give to the service of the community.
5 There is no peace, even after earning much wealth.

FINDING OUT

❶ What did the flags outside the merchant's house represent?

❷ What favour did Guru Nanak ask of the merchant?

❸ What lesson was Guru Nanak trying to teach the merchant?

❹ Write the story from the merchant's point of view. What effect do you think his meeting with Guru Nanak would have had on him?

❺ Read the five Sikh teachings about wealth:

a) In statement 1 wealth is seen as a good thing. Why is this?
b) According to statement 2 how can Sikhs find the Path of Truth?
c) What warnings do statements 3 and 5 contain?
d) How much should a Sikh earning £15,000 a year give to the service of the community? Approximately how much is it a week?

MAKING CONNECTIONS

❶ Working in pairs, think of a famous person you know about who is very wealthy. Carry out research on the person. How did he/she make their wealth? What possessions do they have? Can you find any evidence that they use their wealth to help others?

❷

Celebrity spent nearly ¼ million pounds in a one-day shopping spree

Do you know of a celebrity who has done something like this?

❸ Working in pairs or small groups, carry out some research into wealth and poverty in Scotland. For example, do an Internet search such as 'average income in Scotland'.

❹ When the information from different groups has been pulled together, prepare a report entitled 'Wealth and Poverty in Scotland'.

Thinking it over

① Do you think people set out with the intention of become rich or does it happen more by chance? Do you think becoming rich requires special talents or can anyone become rich?

② What do you think is meant by the 'Path of Truth'? In Sikhism the path of truth is linked with the sharing of wealth. What does this tell you about the Sikh religion?

③

> I wish I'd never won (£5 million lottery winner)

Some people find it hard to cope with sudden riches. What might have happened to make someone wish they hadn't won? Would you rather have lots of money or a happy family life?

④ 'There is no peace, even after earning much wealth.' What do you think this means? Do you think it is true? Why/why not?

⑤

> Belfast woman scoops £20 million

Do you envy the woman from Belfast? Why/why not? What advice would you give her to make sure she remains contented and happy?

⑥ What do you think of the Sikh view that wealth is a good thing because it can be used for charitable purposes?

⑦ Should rich people be forced to share their wealth through higher taxes or should it be voluntary? Give reasons for your answer.

 stimulus 2   The banquet

Guru Nanak spent a lot of time travelling, meeting people and teaching them about God and how to live a good life. After one journey he decided to rest for a few days and stayed at the house of a hard-working carpenter called Lalo. Although Lalo was poor he shared his simple food with Nanak.

In the same village lived a rich man called Malik. When Malik heard that Guru Nanak was in the village he decided to have a large banquet to which he invited Guru Nanak. The day of the banquet arrived. Lots of people came, but there was no sign of Guru Nanak. Malik was angry at this and he sent his servants to ask Guru Nanak to come to the banquet. Nanak went with the servants.

Malik met him and asked him, 'Why didn't you come to my feast? I have rich cake for you, much better than the bread you will get at Lalo's house.'

Guru Nanak said nothing. He took a piece of bread he had brought from Lalo's house and a piece of cake that was on the table at Malik's feast. He squeezed them both. From the bread came a few drops of milk but from the rich cake came some drops of blood. He said to Malik, 'you see Lalo's bread was bought with money earned by honest working. But your cake and all your wealth has come from cheating the poor and living dishonestly.' From that day Malik changed his ways and followed the teaching of Guru Nanak.

Kirat karna

Earning a living through honest work is called kirat karna. In Sikhism work is no less important than worship. Anyone who wastes their time or who shows no interest in working for a living is strongly condemned. Sikhism emphasises that it is important to put effort into life and as far as possible not be dependent on others.

FINDING OUT

1 Who did Guru Nanak stay with in the village?

2 What did Malik do when he heard that Guru Nanak was living in the village?

3 Why was Malik angry?

4 What did he say to Guru Nanak when he met him?

5 What did Nanak do with the bread from Lalo's house and the cake from Malik's table?

6 What did he say to Malik?

7 What is kirat karna? Why do Sikhs think it is important?

MAKING CONNECTIONS

1 Describe an occasion when you or someone you know behaved:

a) honestly.
b) dishonestly.

2 **Poor pensioner cheated out of money by building contractor**

Describe a situation you know about where someone was, or suspects they were, overcharged for work done.

3 Do you know anyone who is often lazy? Have you ever been lazy? What makes people lazy?

4 How does the story illustrate kirat karna? Make up your own story to illustrate kirat karna.

Thinking it over

1 What do people mean when they say 'honesty is the best policy'? Do you think it is true? Can you think of a situation when honesty might not be the best policy?

2 What do you think are the most important jobs in society? Should the most important jobs be the highest paid? Why/why not?

3 'People who refuse to work should not be given money by the government to live on.' Do you agree? Why/why not?

stimulus
3

The marathon runner

Fauja Singh enjoys marathon running. He runs nine or 10 miles a day, every day, clocking up 70 miles a week. What is unusual about Fauja Singh is that he is 93 years old.

After living most of his life in Punjab in India, where he was a farmer, he came to Redbridge in Essex after his wife's death, to join his youngest son and his family. He first saw the London marathon on television after his arrival in Britain and fancied having a go. In all, he has done six marathons – four in London and one each in Toronto and New York. When he runs in London on April 18, he is hoping to come in below the six-hour mark – having crossed the finishing line last year in six hours, two minutes and 43 seconds. Fauja is intensely competitive and loves the fact that he has beaten the London marathon record for his age group – runners in their 90s – every year. 'He loves being a star,' Harmander, his trainer, says, 'he values being recognised, and he sees it as raising the profile of Sikhs.'

He looks the picture of health. He weighs just eight stone, which, for his height of six feet, is almost nothing. He eats a basic vegetarian Punjabi diet, doesn't drink or smoke and avoids new foods in case they upset his system. A simple man of few desires, Fauja says he is grateful to God for giving him the opportunity and the talent to do what he does. He meditates every morning before training and prays every day, morning and evening.

Currently, he runs for Bliss, a charity that helps premature babies; he sometimes also runs under the banner of the British Heart Foundation in honour of some of his jogging friends who have taken up running, several in marathons, since heart attacks. Late last year, Adidas also signed him up for its Nothing Is Impossible advertising campaign. He won't reveal how much money the deal involves, but says that anything he makes goes to charity.

(*The Guardian*, 6th April 2004)

The three responsibilities

The Gurus taught that there are three responsibilities in life. They are:

Nam Japna   To remember God
Kirat Karna   To earn one's living by honest means
Vand Chhakna   To share one's earnings with less fortunate people

A slogan

PRAY

WORK

GIVE

❶ How successful has Fauja Singh been in marathon running? What is unusual about him?

❷ What circumstances led him to take up marathon running?

❸ What charities is he associated with?

❹ How important is Sikhism in his life? How do you know?

❺ Fauja sees his running as 'raising the profile of Sikhs'. What do you think he means?

❻ Look at the three responsibilities and match each of the words in the slogan to one of the responsibilities.

❼ Improve the slogan by adding drawings to illustrate each responsibility.

❽ Look at the account of the marathon runner. How does Fauja Singh keep the responsibility to 'remember God'?

❾ Although Fauja Singh no longer works for money, how does he keep the responsibility to share his earnings?

MAKING CONNECTIONS

❶ Have you ever raised money by being sponsored to do something? Describe the experience.

❷ Running a marathon must be hard. What's the most difficult thing you have done which has given you a sense of success and achievement?

❸ Think over the last few weeks. Make a list of the things you have done that have given you a feeling of success.

Thinking it over

❶ Do you admire Fauja Singh? Why/why not?

❷ Fauja sees his running as 'raising the profile of Sikhs'. What do you think he means? Do you think he has raised the profile of Sikhs?

❸ 'Fauja Singh is a good example to everybody. He has beliefs and he puts them into practice.' Do you agree? What do you think a non-Sikh might learn from the example of Fauja Singh?

stimulus 4 *A Choice*

The story below is one that is told to Sikh children.

One day a woman came out of her house and saw three old men with beards sitting in her yard. She didn't know them but she thought they looked hungry. She said to them 'You look hungry, come inside and have a bite to eat.' But they declined. When her husband came home, she told him about the three old men.

He said, 'Go outside and tell them to come in'. So she did. However, one of the old man told her that they never went into the house together. He pointed to one man and said 'that's Wealth. My friend over there – he's Success and I am Love. Now go in the house and discuss with your husband and ask which one you would like to come in.

The woman went in and told her husband. He was very pleased. He said, 'Let's invite in Wealth and then we'll never be poor again. But his wife disagreed. 'Let's invite in Success – I've always wanted us to be successful.' But their daughter-in law

disagreed. She said, 'Love would be best. We should fill our home with love.' The family all agreed that the daughter-in-law's advice was best. So they went outside and said to Love, 'we'd like you to come in.'

Love got up and started walking towards the house. Immediately Wealth and Success got up and followed him. The family was surprised. The old man told her, 'If you had invited Wealth or Success, the other two would have stayed out, but since you invited Love – wherever he goes, we go. Wherever there is love, there is also wealth and success.'

FINDING OUT

❶ What values did the three old men represent?

❷ Which old man did the family eventually decide to invite inside? What happened?

❸ What is the message of the story?

MAKING CONNECTIONS

❶ Think of people you know and people you have heard about in the media. Name
a person you know who is wealthy
a person you think is successful
a person who shows love in the way they live their life.

In each case explain why you chose that person. Produce a class list of people under these headings: Wealthy, Successful, Loving. Do any people appear on more than one list? Have a class debate to identify the three people from the list who have made the greatest contribution to society.

Thinking it over

❶ Which would you have chosen – wealth, success or love? Explain your choice.

❷ Do you agree with Sikhism that 'wherever there is love, there is also wealth and success'? Give reasons for your answer.

❸ Is success always associated with wealth? What makes you say that?

❹ Wealth and success are sometimes accompanied by 'ruthlessness'. Why do you think this is? Is wealth or success gained through ruthlessness to be admired or not? Give reasons for your answer.

❺ 'Nothing succeeds like success.' What do you think this means? Do you think it is true? Why/why not?

❻ How important is it to be successful in whatever you do? What makes you say that? Does it matter if sometimes you are not successful?

stimulus 5 *Pingalwara*

Pingalwara is an organisation set up to help people in need. It was founded by a Sikh, Bhagat Puran Singh and is based upon Sikh principles, especially the principle of 'sewa', meaning service.

Bhagat Puran Singh (1904–1992)

Founder of Pingalwara

Bhagat Puran Singh
(1904 - 1992)

Every society has its share of individuals who are sick, disabled, suffering and deserted by mankind. There are old people and newborn babies no one wants to look after. There are disabled people who are not admitted into any of the hospitals and are left to die at the roadside. There are diseased persons no one wants to touch.

Who is to look after them?

This question was asked by the founder of Pigalwara, Bhagat Puran Singh.

As a young man, Bhagat Puran Singh saw in Lahore the suffering and the misery of many people, often abandoned by their families. Inspired by the teaching of the Sikh Gurus he resolved to put into practice the Sikh belief in sewa, serving others.

His work began when he came across a forsaken, disabled child, suffering from polio. For the next 14 years he carried this boy around. His aim was to develop a place of healing and treatment for such people, where they could be part of a family. He would accept anybody to the community regardless of their caste, belief, religion, or community.

The work of Pingalwara

Providing medicine
Today Pingalwara provides a dispensary where doctors come everyday for voluntary service and provide poor people with free medicine.

Providing education
A school is being run in the slums of Amritsar where free education, books, stationery etc. are provided to the children. A vocational training centre has been set up to teach skills like weaving, candle-making, sewing and embroidery.

Responding to disaster
In August 2004 many of the villages in the district of Sangrur were flooded due to breaches in the river Chaggar. The worst affected were the daily wage earners who were left without food and shelter. A Pingalwara team led by Dr Inderjit Kaur visited the affected areas and provided the urgently required help in the form of rations, clothes and medical aid.

Responding to medical emergencies
Blood is needed for many patients with injuries and fractured bones. This problem has been tackled with the help of Blood Donation Camps organised every year on the eve of the anniversary of Bhagat Puran Singh's death. A trauma van has also been acquired to provide for accident victims.

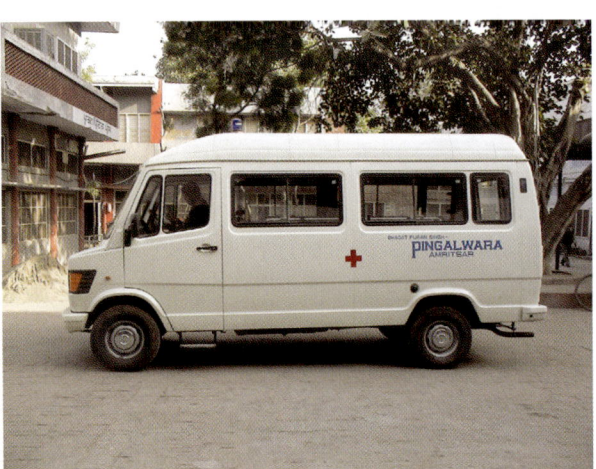

❶ What is 'sewa'?

❷ What experiences led Bhagat Puran Singh to begin his work?

❸ Describe two examples of the work Pingalwara does.

❹ Explain how Pingalwara demonstrates the Sikh belief in Sewa.

❺ Explain how Pingalwara demonstrates the Sikh belief in equality.

❻ Find out more about the work of Pingalwara at www.pingalwaraonline.org.

MAKING CONNECTIONS

❶ Look at the different kinds of work done by Pingalwara. Find other organisations that do similar work.

❷ Pingalwara depends upon the skills of many people. What skills do you have that you could use to help others?

❸ There is much suffering in the world. What could you do to help? Do you think you could make a difference? Make a list of bullet points of what you could do. For ideas look up the website www.vso.org.uk.

Thinking it over

❶ Seeing people suffering, in need and uncared for makes some people ask the question 'Who is to look after them?' What was Bhagat Puran Singh's answer to that question? What is your answer to that question?

❷ Seeing people suffering, in need and uncared for might make some people ask the question 'Why does God allow such suffering to happen?' What is your answer to that question?

Index